A FIRESIDE BOOK

PUBLISHED BY SIMON & SCHUSTER

NEW YORK LONDON TORONTO SYDNEY SINGAPORE

Stepwives

10 Steps to Help Ex-Wives and
Stepmothers End the Struggle
and Put the Kids First

*Lynne Oxhorn-Ringwood
and Louise Oxhorn*

*with Marjorie Vego Krausz,
Ed.D., M.F.T.*

FIRESIDE
Rockefeller Center
1230 Avenue of the Americas
New York, NY 10020

For information regarding special discounts for bulk purchases,
please contact Simon & Schuster Special Sales:
1-800-456-6798 or business@simonandschuster.com

Designed by Diane Hobbing

Manufactured in the United States of America

3 5 7 9 10 8 6 4

Library of Congress Cataloging-in-Publication Data is available.

ISBN 0-7432-2246-6

Acknowledgments

We have been on quite a journey, but before we go any farther, we must thank and acknowledge Marjorie Vego Krausz, Ed.D., our co-author, for her invaluable contributions, not only in helping us develop the program *Stepwives* is based on but in bringing enormous insight to the project as she helped us delve deeper into the conflicts stepwives face. She has been with us every step of the way, and, through the different phases and roads we've traveled, there are many others that we must thank.

First . . . to Evan . . . to Greg . . . to Paul and Jared . . . to Howard, Brian, and Sean, our families, the loves of our lives, whose love, support, and wisdom fill us with unending joy: thank you for being there for us throughout this project and through all our endeavors. We cherish every moment we are together and are so thankful to have you all in our lives.

To our family and friends—always there, always loving: thank you for your encouragement and unconditional love.

To Angela Rinaldi, our agent and friend, who believed in us right from the start: thank you. To our editor, Trish Todd, who helped us realize our dreams and desires to help other families, and to Marcia Burch and Lisa Sciambra, who helped us get our message out there: thank you. Our gratitude goes to Ellen Fein for sending us in the right direction. To Stedman Mays, thank you for all of your time, encouragement, and advice. To Michael Crawford and our entire "office staff" at Charlie's, our favorite seaside restaurant in Cardiff: we can't thank you enough for always welcoming us and allowing us to meet there. Our appreciation goes to Susan Dunsworth, the Webmommy, for her creativity, generosity, and warm spirit. Special thanks to David Levy of the Children's Rights Council for his constant support, and to Jacquie Cohen for her hard work and creativity in public relations and for helping establish the CoMamas program at Jewish Family Service of San Diego. To Judge Domnitz of San Diego Superior Court: we thank you for believing in our program. We also extend our thanks to Mike Sirota for his help with editing and to Donna Frazier Glynn for getting our creative juices flowing. Our heartfelt gratitude goes to our CoMamas volunteers, Leslie Leinbach and Katie Strand, for their tireless efforts on behalf of the Association and stepwives everywhere. And last, but not least, to The Children and all of the stepwives who have shared their stories and opened their hearts to us, we say: we couldn't have done it without you.

Dedication

This book is dedicated to Evan, whose inherent sense of self-respect helped us always try to put him first (no matter how we felt about each other), whose sacrifices as a child of divorce and remarriage inspired us to create the CoMamas movement, and whose generosity of spirit allowed us to open up our lives and share our story with the world in the hope of making life better for children everywhere. We love you, Evan.

Contents

Introduction

Stepmother. Ex-wife. Just the words are enough to make anybody roll their eyes, take a deep breath, and offer their condolences. But no matter which one you are, stepmother or ex-wife, once you've assumed one of these roles, the two of you are in each other's lives, for better or for worse. What exactly is your relationship?

To date, no name has been given to this relationship that millions of women are involved in. To answer this need, we've created the word *stepwife*. And since you're reading this book, you are probably a stepwife yourself, trying to make sense of the confusion caused when two women have been married to the same man.

We are stepwives: the ex-wife and current wife of the same man, mother and stepmother to the same child, destined to drag each other through the happiest and saddest occasions life presents. We've even been cursed with the same initials.

Had you asked us even a few years ago if we would ever willingly be in the same room, let alone write an entire book together, our answer would have been a simultaneous, "No way!" We were two women who loathed each other, locked in an intense battle for power and position for over a decade. Even after Lynne married Paul, our situation still did not get better. There seemed to be no way out.

Through it all, somehow we managed to put our (step)son, Evan, first, rarely behaving badly in front of him. In fact, teachers and parents would continually remark on just how civilized we were, how well adjusted he was. Little did they realize it was a completely different story behind closed doors. Then we let each other know just what our true feelings were and how much we hated being in each other's lives.

The stepwife relationship is ongoing and inescapable. No matter what you do, your stepwife is here to stay. And although we cannot make her go away, we can help you figure out how to handle having her in your life, even if it feels hopeless, even if you've been embroiled in an ugly battle for many years. It is never too late for it to get better.

Our book looks at this life from both sides: two women struggling to raise a child together in two different homes. We've opened up our private lives and the lives of others like us. Any woman who has ever heard the word *stepmother* or *ex-wife* will find this compelling reading. As we share the dimensions of our conflict, from the anger to the acceptance, mothers and stepmothers will appreciate that although they too may collide, they need not shatter. In fact, they can move beyond life as they now know it into a whole new world: the world of CoMamas—women who have learned to co-parent in a healthy, respectful manner.

So how did we do it? The miracle happened when one of us called the other to apologize after another battle. In that brief moment of truce, we found we actually agreed on something: Our situation had become unbearable, and we needed to change it.

To confirm our suspicions that other stepwives were also battling, we developed a Web site. Thousands of women all over the world have visited our site and told us their own horror stories about their stepwives. Their stories helped us and psychologist and marriage/family therapist Marjorie Krausz develop our step-by-step program, the PRESCRP-TON, and later consult privately with stepwives and their men, conduct seminars and support groups, and write this book.

As the book evolved, with Dr. Krausz's help, we began understanding more and more about what makes the stepwife connection so inherently difficult. To begin with, you're predisposed to dislike each other, and it's usually downhill from there. But no matter how bad your situation is, we encourage you not to give up hope, because even if you think your stepwife would never work with you, you can still work our program alone. When you change the way you respond to your stepwife over time, *you* will change the dynamics of your relationship over time.

We now feel grateful for the insights we have gained, for helping each other fit some very important missing pieces into the puzzle of our lives. As we continue to heal, we rejoice in the knowledge that rather than living with an enemy, we each have an ally, someone with whom we can cooperate rather than argue. We have become CoMamas. And when we look into the future, to that inevitable day when we both get to answer to that sweet little voice calling, "Grandma?" we know we don't have to be afraid anymore.

So whether you're a divorced mother with a stepwife, a mother contemplating divorce, a stepmother, or planning to marry a man who has children, we are confident this book will help you. Let us guide you as you attempt to navigate the bumpy road ahead, for we have traveled that very same road. And although we still encounter bumps along the way, they are now few and far between. Follow us. Our advice is sound, our directions clear, and, most important, our son, Evan, is happy and very well adjusted. If we can do it, so can you.

THE CHILDREN'S
BILL OF RIGHTS

Adopted from Putting Kids First: Walking Away from a
Marriage Without Walking over the Kids *by Michael
Oddenino, attorney for Children's Rights Council*

We feel that all children of divorce are entitled to these
   rights:
The right to be treated as important human beings and
   not as a source of argument for parents.
The right to a continuing relationship with both parents and the freedom to receive love from and express love for both.
The right to express love for each parent without having to stifle that love because of fear of disapproval
   from the other parent.
The right to know that their parents' decision to divorce
   is not their responsibility and that they will still be
   able to live with each parent.
The right to honest answers to questions about changing family relationships.
The right to know and appreciate what is good in each
   parent without one parent degrading the other.
The right to have a relaxed, secure relationship with
   both parents without being placed in a position to
   manipulate one parent against the other.
The right to have one parent not undermine time with
   the other parent.
The right to be able to experience regular and consistent parental contact.
The right to be a kid and be insulated from the conflict
   and problems of the parents.

Stepwives

Chapter 1

The Same Shoes

Nineteen years ago in the small town of Santa Monica, just northwest of Los Angeles, a baby boy was born. As his mother, Lynne, held him in her arms on that very first day of his life, seized by the most tremendous outpouring of love she had ever known, she experienced a premonition that took years to understand:

> *As I gazed lovingly at my beautiful son, I knew, as surely as I knew my own name, that someday some woman would come between us. "Aha!" I thought. "His future wife!" Feeling safe from this danger for many years to come, I tossed that nasty thought right out of my head and resumed marveling at the perfect miracle before me. Little did I know as I sat with my treasured newborn son that "someday" would come around much sooner than I had anticipated and that it would not be his wife that would cause the pain. It would be his stepmother, Louise.*

When Louise was a little girl she dreamed the dream most little girls dream: of a handsome prince who would someday make her a princess:

> *I pictured our life together, just the two of us, living happily ever after, nothing marring our perfect existence. Oh, maybe one day we would have children, but that would only enhance our lives. How could I have imagined that the child in my life would be someone else's and that*

> *his mother would come as part of that same package, shattering my childhood dream?*

In the beginning, *enemies* was too kind a word to describe what we were to each other. Lynne is Greg's first wife. Louise is the woman who replaced her. Although we shared the care of Lynne's son, Evan, we were so threatened, resentful, and jealous of each other that it took two years after Louise came into the picture for us finally to meet.

It's still amazing to us that we ever ended our decade-long war. Very little that had come before gave any clue that peace was possible, or even desirable. Like meteors destined to collide, our fate was determined long before we actually met. We'd married the same guy, which meant he'd found something to love in each of us. And at the core, that was the problem. What if Greg went back to Lynne? What if the love they had shared was stronger than the love that had developed between Louise and Greg? For Lynne, Louise was the obstacle that stood in the way of her and Greg's making their way back to each other so they could be a family again. At any given moment, one of us felt like the victor, one the vanquished. Maybe the new relationship would turn out to be a mistake, a blip on the screen before true love reasserted itself. Or maybe the new relationship would take root, obliterating the past, and the role of stepmom would eclipse the role of mother. Either way, it was impossible to settle into our altered roles and just skate on with our lives. It was more like Roller Derby—each of us always conscious of the competitor trying to elbow us out of the picture.

Our history together starts with what we think of as the denial era. Although we knew, in some unacknowledged corner of our minds, that life was carrying us into each other's orbits, we chose to ignore it. When Louise came on the scene, it had been less than a year since Lynne and Greg had split up, and Lynne was struggling to make sense of the mess her life had become. She was grief stricken over the loss of her family and the life she had known for fifteen years, and it was more painful than she had ever imagined it could be. At least as the mother of Evan, now 5 years old, she was still enjoying her position as the most influential woman in Greg's life, and when Louise and Greg started dating, nothing much seemed to change. After all, Greg had dated other women, and look who was still here: Lynne, Greg, and Evan.

For Louise, Lynne was a looming presence who seemed ready to pounce at any moment and reclaim her life. But when you really fall in love—especially when it doesn't happen until you're almost thirty years old—you become almost entirely single-minded. And since no one was rushing to make introductions, Louise did what any other normal red-blooded woman in love would do: she pretended Greg's ex-wife didn't exist. She managed to overlook one small detail, however: as Evan's mother, Lynne came along with the package, and Louise would eventually have to reckon with her.

Is it any wonder we didn't want to meet each other? For Louise, meeting Lynne would mean coming face to face with Greg's past, a past that didn't really feel like a past at all, and it would be just one more reminder that she wasn't his one and only. What Louise could never understand, though, was why Lynne didn't want to meet her. Shouldn't a mother want to meet the woman who was going to be such a big part of her child's life? Something was definitely wrong here.

As for Lynne, she was in her own world of denial, hoping and praying that the inevitable would not come to pass—

that Evan would not have a stepmother, that Greg would not have a new wife, that someone she didn't know and did not choose would be part of the family she had created. All she could think about was how Louise was pushing her way into her life.

These were the mind-sets that fueled the hundreds of small fires that had burned us repeatedly before we ever even met, twisting the other person's words and intentions far beyond recognition.

Lynne remembers one such incident this way:

> *Everyone knows it never rains in California—at least it hadn't for many months. We were coming off a three-month drought, and early one morning I awoke to pouring rain, worried sick that Evan had no rain gear at his dad's. Since we had been sharing his little gray jacket and it was at my house, I called to say I would drop it off on my way to work. BL [Before Louise] this had been standard operating procedure, but the response that greeted me when Louise answered set me straight. Things had changed, and now I was no longer in charge of what went on in my own child's life, even though he was only six years old.*

Louise remembers the same incident this way:

> *It was a cold rainy day—the kind Californians are completely unprepared for, and I was no different. The rain made everyone uptight and nervous—as if I weren't nervous enough. Greg had gone out of town on business, and for the very first time I would be solely responsible for getting Evan off to school. The shrill ringing of the phone*

startled me—the last thing I needed at 6:30 a.m. It was
Lynne calling to notify me that she was on her way over
to drop off a jacket for Evan. Was she kidding? Did she
honestly think we would send Evan to school without a
jacket on a rainy day? How insulting.

We were prime examples of how stepwives can miscon-
strue any situation, never giving each other the benefit of
the doubt and always assuming the other is intentionally
trying to push you aside. We always brought out each
other's lower selves—Lynne feeling like the ex-wife whose
territory was constantly being trampled and Louise feeling
insecure over what exactly her role was.

Two years passed before we ever met face to face, but we
felt each other's presence in a million different ways.
Against this emotional background we prepared for the
showdown that was to be our first meeting—not that either
of us really wanted to meet. But how could we avoid it? There
was no escaping the fact that we were going to be raising the
same child together for longer than either of us cared to
admit. We were opponents in the truest sense of the word:
wary, cautious, and extremely distrustful of each other. And
when the day arrived, we played out the roles that came
most naturally to us. Neither of us came in with a plan; we
were driven instead by the fatalistic sense that both pro-
pelled and repelled us.

Lynne:

When I arrived at the restaurant, I looked around the
parking lot and didn't see her car. I knew it well because it

had once been mine. My palms were sweating, and I was so nervous I could barely breathe. I felt my insides turn to mush. Positioned where I could see the door, I watched for her. I had never even seen a picture of her, but something told me I would recognize her when I saw her.

As the customers filed in, I made mental notes. I waited and watched until I spotted her. Fashionably dressed. Thin. Long dark hair. And looking as nervous as I felt. When I noticed her hands shaking, I wasn't afraid anymore. Thinking about how vulnerable she looked and having been there first, I felt compelled to warn her of the pitfalls she would surely encounter once married. I let her know that Greg and I had once been very much in love and that she needed to be careful, because that was no guarantee: look what had happened to us. I listened as she spoke of her insecurities at not being his one and only, and that evening, for the first and perhaps the last time for a very long time, I felt what she must be going through. I remembered how special was the young love I had once shared with her man, and so by the end of that evening—for that one evening—I no longer hated her. I understood her. But the glow of the evening was not to last.

Louise:

I'd been dreading the meeting all week, yet I was filled with a sort of morbid curiosity. What would she be like in the flesh? I'd heard so much about her (hardly any of it good), yet couldn't quite get a handle on what she would actually be like. As I entered the restaurant, I could feel beads of sweat slowly trickling down my back—and then

I spotted her. I had seen her picture, but I would have known her anywhere.

We looked each other over. She began right away: "You probably want to know all about the woman Greg had been in love with." Now why would she think that? I felt my heart slowly start to sink, and by the time she was through with me, I thought I'd have to pick myself up off the floor. I heard it all. How they'd met in college, children of the sixties and sooo much in love. In fact, they hadn't had so much as a single argument for the first five years of their marriage. As if that weren't bad enough, somehow she managed to shift gears, and things got even worse. I got the lowdown on what I could expect from my future with Greg, and it wasn't exactly pretty. She had been there, she warned, and felt the need to share her experiences as the older, wiser first wife, almost as if she were doing me a favor.

Well, if I didn't like her before, I liked her even less now. Was she trying to ruin my life? As we said our good-bys, I hoped I would never have to lay eyes on her again. But what was I thinking? I'd be seeing her plenty. After all, she was Evan's mother.

Each of us tried to shake off the raw feelings of pain and get on with things. What good would there be in staying stuck in the confusion of what we were feeling? It wasn't that either of us thought that the other had personally intervened to ruin our dreams of what life was supposed to be like. It was more circumstantial: feel the pain, look up, and the tracks lead back to you know who. For Lynne, it was a short hop from "I gave up everything" to "I blew it." And for Louise, there was the complex feeling of having gotten more and less than she bargained for. The freshness of her start with Greg, of love at last, was somehow tainted by the fact that his ex-wife came along as part of the deal.

Louise shares the news of her proposal with Lynne:

> *Every unmarried girl who is still breathing longs to hear the words, "Will you marry me?" And if you're the second wife, you can't wait for wife number one to know that her reign is officially over.*
>
> *Thinking this might be a good time for Lynne and me to put our bad feelings aside and start over, I called her. But she couldn't have been any clearer. She wanted nothing to do with me, now or ever. I guess I shouldn't have been surprised. What I couldn't understand, though, was why she was so upset to have me in her life when she was the one who had wanted out of her marriage. As distasteful as it was, there was no changing the fact that I was stuck with her now.*

According to Lynne, it happened this way:

> *Of course, everyone in my life knew who the infamous Louise was. She had been the topic of many a late-night phone call, early-morning coffee klatch, or evening cocktail party. And now, here she was on the phone, calling on a Sunday morning . . . perhaps to discuss the weather?*
>
> *"Hello, Lynne," she said in that voice of hers. "This is Louise. I know we've had our problems in the past, but I was just calling to see if we couldn't try and patch things*

> up between us, because," she said, hardly containing her
> joy, "Greg and I are getting married! And now I'm gonna
> be around for a long, long time."
>
> A fate worse than death! I couldn't possibly imagine
> anything worse than being sentenced to having this
> woman in my life one day longer, let alone 'til death do us
> part.

As the wedding approached, Lynne's feelings of powerlessness increased. Her deep fear of being replaced was becoming a reality, and it compounded the force of her negative thoughts toward Louise. And in the midst of prenuptial bliss, Louise was having intermittent feelings of panic and anxiety over marrying a man with so much baggage. Lynne had robbed her of her dream of a perfect life, and she couldn't ignore the fact that Lynne would indeed have an impact on her.

We couldn't help but be full of "if onlys," and every "if only" was filled not only with regret but consternation as well. Even for the most evolved human, it's not all that easy to face questions like, "Have I ruined my life?" and "What have I done?" And we weren't exactly evolved in our thinking toward each other.

If only Lynne had stayed married to Greg. If only Louise had met him first. If only Lynne had met him when she was older. If only Louise had met him when she was younger. The truth, of course, is that things happened exactly as they were meant to. Meeting the right person at the right time is something most of us hope destiny will provide. It just so happened that our destiny was with the same man, albeit at different times.

• • •

Lynne's journal entry from October 21, 1990:

The weekend Louise and Greg got married were the two worst days of my life . . . up to that point, anyway. The wedding was the last thing I wanted to think about, but I kept seeing them in my mind: she in a beautiful long white gown and he in a tux.

When their wedding day dawned bright and sunny, it felt as if Mother Nature had conspired against me. I tried to hide my emotions but just couldn't prevent myself from feeling I'd lost everything that had ever been important: my husband, my family, my friends, my home, my possessions, my security, my position in life's pecking order. And the minute they said I do, she would be in my life forever. Leaving Greg had been my choice, but I was devastated that he had found someone else so soon.

As the hour approached the fateful moment, I withdrew further into my own thoughts, picturing her there at the altar . . . with my husband. My precious son would be up there with them, sharing in their happiness. Evan wouldn't be part of my grief. They had more to offer him. I was just a single mom now, struggling to make ends meet, fighting to build a new life with little emotional support from anyone. I felt at that moment as if I had lost my son to her too. And I was powerless to stop yet another torrent of tears.

Louise's wedding day memories:

My wedding day had finally arrived—and it was a perfect day. The sun was shimmering on the ocean, which was that indescribable color somewhere between dark blue and deep green. A harpist was playing in the background, champagne was flowing, and all our family and friends were there.

Evan, the best man, walked down the aisle first, followed by his dad, the groom. As Greg made his way toward the altar, all our guests, as if on cue, stood and began to cheer. Suddenly, it was my turn. As "Here Comes the Bride" began to play, I felt a tingling sensation throughout my entire body and practically ran toward them. And when I said "I do," standing next to Greg and Evan, I was filled with the most powerful sense of elation I'd ever known.

When I entered the reception room, the party was in full swing. I walked out onto the dance floor and immediately looked for Evan. As I stood in the midst of my wedding wearing the most exquisite wedding gown imaginable and feeling like Cinderella at the ball, I finally spotted him. I opened my arms wide for him to come and dance with me—and he wouldn't. I found myself rooted to the spot, devastated, willing myself not to cry. In that instant, the reality of marrying a man who had been married before came crashing down on me. Maybe we wouldn't be one big, happy family. Maybe my new life wouldn't be so perfect after all.

The lines had been drawn for real now, and there was no way out for either of us. You'd think we would've reached a neutral peace by then, but things had gotten worse over the last three years instead of better. It's not as if we hadn't tried, over and over, to get along. We'd met, we'd talked, and we had tried to figure out how to make room for both of us in the confining space being stepwives had relegated us to.

But the truth was that we brought out the worst in each other and didn't know how to get along.

Lynne didn't feel depressed or self-pitying all the time—far from it. But Louise was a trigger, a mood changer. One look at her face, and Lynne suddenly felt like an outsider in her own life. So what if she'd built a great new life for herself? Louise had the magical ability to make her ache for what she'd lost.

Louise was thoroughly enjoying her new life. The role of wife and stepmother fit her to a tee, and at times she *almost* forgot about Lynne—that persistent dark cloud that hovered over her life, threatening to rain down on her whenever she least expected it.

Our relationship was built on thousands of difficult moments that stung like sand in the face. Sometimes the pain was intense, sometimes just a quick stab, but the undercurrent of feeling was always the same. Someone got there first. Someone snatched away what you wanted. Someone dragged her hand across the perfect picture you'd had for your life and smeared it into something unrecognizable. And all we wanted was for that someone to go away. But of course that was not to be.

The question everyone asks us is: How could we possibly have put aside so many years of bitterness, envy, and fighting to finally begin the healing process? It was the Shoe Incident, in Year 10 of our standoff, that finally helped us push open the doors we'd slammed shut in our relationship.

Lynne:

I had always thought of Louise as my punishment for getting divorced—a kind of instant karma that simply would not go away. Not only had Louise become part of a clique that included the parents of Evan's friends—leaving me persona non grata at all school events; to top it all off: she had become best friends with members of my own family. I felt as if she were stealing my very identity. I had rebuilt my life, I was happily married, and my son was doing beautifully, but my feelings toward her remained the same: I thought of her as an intruder in my life, and I hated her with a vengeance.

Evan had been begging relentlessly for a dog, and when he was eleven, I did what any other mother would do: I agreed to get him one, but only if Greg and Louise would dog-sit when we were out of town. We went out and adopted Sammy, a sweet little dog with big brown eyes, long droopy ears, a curled-up tail, and a crooked, snaggle-toothed smile, and over the years Greg and Louise kept him several times. I guess I wasn't really surprised when Louise decided that she would get a dog too. She didn't go as far as naming him Sammy, probably because he already had a name: Simon. But of course, she gave him a nickname. And, of course, it was Simey.

I saw Simey for the first time when Louise brought him over for me to dog-sit. I wasn't in a great mood. I'd just found out that another longtime friend of mine was joining ranks with Louise, and I was less than polite when she stepped out of the car to say hello. Then I saw Simey. He looked just like Sammy: big brown eyes, long droopy ears, a curled-up tail, and even a crooked, snaggle-toothed smile. Imagine my disgust when I saw that all of his doggie paraphernalia was exactly like Sammy's. I thought I was going to scream.

I really lost it, though, when I glanced down, and my eye caught something even more familiar. Louise was wearing the same shoes I had on. *I knew this was no coincidence. I'd had these shoes for two years, and I wore them all the time. She'd seen me in them. Did she think we were the Bobbsey Twins or something? I couldn't keep quiet any longer. I looked her in the face and demanded, "Why are you wearing those shoes?!"*

Louise:

I arrived at Lynne's to drop off my dog, not knowing what to expect. I never really knew how she'd act when she saw me. Mostly she made a point of ignoring me, but occasionally she'd throw me off by being somewhat friendly. I walked a fine line with her and usually managed to cross it.

I was a little nervous about leaving my dog, Simey, my baby, with the enemy, but it seemed better than a kennel.

She kept us waiting, and when she finally appeared, she took one look at Simey and me. The first words out of her mouth were, "Why are you wearing those shoes?" It seemed we were wearing the very same shoes.

"What?" I asked warily.

"I've had these shoes for years, and now you have them too," she snapped.

Oh no, not again! *I thought as I gritted my teeth. Not that same old crap about me having her life. She seemed to believe I wanted to be just like her and that anything I had was a direct result of my trying to take what was her's. But this time she'd gone too far. Did she think she* had a corner on the shoe market too? I'd had my shoes for two years, just like her, and I was going to wear them whenever I felt like it.

I petted Simey nervously while I tried to regain my composure and concentrate on the more immediate problem at hand. I was supposed to leave my precious dog in this woman's care for two and a half weeks. I wasn't sure I should do it, but what other choice did I have?

I got Simey's stuff out of the trunk and reluctantly handed him over to her. "Be good and have a good time," I said to the door that slammed as they disappeared into her house.

I seethed all the way home. It was always going to be like this. We really had made no progress in our relationship in all these years. Something had to change, but after ten years, what could?

It was no wonder that the first thing Simey did when she put him down in the house was pee on her rug. I think he'd felt her hostility toward me and behaved accordingly—and who could blame him?

While Louise was gone, we each brooded about how miserable our lives had become. For Lynne, who had a very badly behaved house guest, the days stretched on forever. It seemed that whenever she turned her back, Simon peed again, as if claiming her house as Louise's territory. Louise spent those same weeks worried sick about her dog, wondering how Lynne was treating Simey. As she laced up The Shoes each day, she fumed. "When is Lynne going to get that this is my life?" Even thousands of miles away from each other, we were inexplicably connected and couldn't escape the box our lives had become.

Two and a half torturous weeks later when Louise came to pick up Simon, our anxiety had reached a new high. We weren't sure how the other would react, and maybe our guilt, or the gnawing feeling that we'd hit rock-bottom, made us a little more open to what came next. As Louise reached for her beloved dog, relieved to find him alive and well, she apologized to Lynne for having the same shoes. It was just a few words, but they were our turning point. In that brief moment, it felt as if the revolving door we had been stuck in had finally released us.

Somehow we had managed to pause and see important details we'd been missing about ourselves and each other. When Lynne heard Louise apologize about the shoes, she realized they hadn't been fighting about shoes at all. Tired of feeling rotten, she decided to expose her feelings and tell Louise what she had been dying to say for years, and why not? There was clearly nothing to lose: "When I looked down and saw those shoes on your feet, it reminded me that everything I once had is now yours. Nothing feels like it's just mine anymore—not my life, not my stuff, not even my own child. And over the years, that feeling has just gotten worse. So when you showed up wearing my favorite shoes—shoes I'd never seen on anyone else—it felt like just one more thing I had to share with you, and I couldn't take it anymore. I had to say something."

Louise listened dumbstruck. How could Lynne actually think she had liked following in her footsteps to become Greg's second wife or that she enjoyed having Lynne's old crap in her house? The first words out of her mouth were: "Do you really think my dream was to become a second wife, saddled with another woman's stuff?" But that wasn't her only thought. Louise was actually starting to get a sense of what it must have been like for Lynne to have to give up her child every other week to a woman she barely knew and didn't even like. If Louise had felt this much anxiety over leaving her dog with Lynne, what must Lynne have felt every time Evan left her to be at his dad's? She'd never been able to put herself in Lynne's place before, and the new feeling of empathy left her surprised and almost hopeful that maybe things really could get better—this time.

Lynne wondered how she had missed something so obvious as a second wife's not wanting her stepwife's hand-me-downs. Why would any woman want to live in another woman's shadow? She found herself empathizing with Louise just a little, and in a sudden rush of understanding she was unwilling to put aside, she apologized too.

There are apologies, and then there are apologies, but this one had been based on mutual empathy, something entirely foreign to us as stepwives, and even though it felt strange, we wanted to hold on to it. It was as if we had been hit over the head with a two-by-four. Somehow we'd never managed to see that the other person was suffering and that she wasn't getting what *she* wanted either. We had been seeing only our own situation through lenses distorted by jealousy and pain. Maybe it wasn't the other person's fault after all. Could it be that each of us had been wrong?

As ridiculous as it sounds, our lives would be forever changed by the simple act of choosing the same shoes, much as they were transformed by having chosen the same man. On closer inspection, the infamous strappy sandals were similar but not exactly the same, a fact we were soon to find out about each other too. That day we discovered we had each been writing, and stacks of unsent letters, journal entries, unfinished stories, and poems had been piling up over the years, just waiting to be read. Now that our private ravings had been revealed, our curiosity was running rampant. And although we were terrified by how we would find ourselves portrayed, the truth was that we were each dying for a peek at the juicy details the other had written. So we mustered up our courage and decided to get together again, this time armed with years of "documentation," and see where it would take us.

Lynne began, "All you've ever heard about my life with Greg was the bad stuff, and over the years, you've examined all my dirty laundry. How do you think that feels? I guess it's just important to me to have you acknowledge that I'm not just 'the crazy ex-wife.' I want you to know that I'm a person with feelings too, and believe it or not, people usually like me."

Deciding to let it all hang out, Louise answered honestly, "I just can't help feeling jealous. When you and Greg were first together, all you had to think about was each other and being in love. When I met him, he was gun-shy. And thanks to you, he had lots of things to focus on other than me. All I really wanted was his undivided love and attention just like you had—and I was never going to have that."

"You know, Louise," Lynne said falteringly, "I thought what Greg and I had was special, but when I hear about the two of you, I can't help but wonder if all those years I spent with him were just a lie. How do you think it feels when I realize I was so easy to replace?"

"Well, it wasn't as if there weren't reminders of you all over the place," Louise replied heatedly. "How do you think it feels to be somewhere and have someone call you by your stepwife's name? And then dead silence as everyone realizes the mistake. And you're left reassuring them that it's no big deal, when you really just want to scream, '*I'm not her.*' "

For the first time, Louise was beginning to see where some of her hostility toward Lynne had come from, and she saw that it wasn't entirely Lynne's fault after all. Lynne couldn't change the fact that she was the one who married Greg first. And Lynne began to see that it really wasn't Louise's fault that she came along when she did and that maybe Louise didn't deserve her animosity.

As we spoke, we had a revelation: it was amazing how many of the issues that had come up between us weren't strictly personal; they were built into our situation. Certainly we have to admit we made it all worse with our anything but saintly behavior, but almost any ex-wife would feel discarded, whether or not the woman who replaced her had anything to do with the demise of her marriage. And almost any second wife was bound to feel regrets about not being first.

Because the stepwife relationship isn't one you choose, there's almost none of the usual process of giving the other person a chance or getting to know her over time, so it is unlikely that you will casually start chatting and eventually discover each other as people. But it doesn't matter. Whether you've been a stepwife for one year or ten, by shifting your perception of your stepwife and examining how your situation looks and feels to her, you can begin the process of changing your relationship. It doesn't have to take you more than a decade like it did us. You can accelerate the process we blundered our way through by learning not only from our mistakes but from our successes as well.

What we found was that it was our developing empathy that allowed us to change our behavior. Empathy is something you can develop on your own when you finally step outside your own behavior and see your stepwife's point of view. And when you decide to change your behavior, you will find, over time, that your stepwife will respond differently to you.

Deepening levels of understanding and changing behavior is what has worked for others and if you try it, you may find that it works for you too—it certainly took us from stepwives to CoMamas. By giving up the notion that our own individual perceptions were reality, we were able to have a dialogue with each other instead of a monologue. We were able to listen instead of simply wanting to be heard. Make no mistake about it—it wasn't easy. By questioning our own motivations, we were on what felt like very shaky ground, and to us it felt as though that ground could give way at any moment and we would be left hanging. The one certainty we clung to was that if we wanted things to continue moving in a positive direction, we had to keep working at it. Our lives and the lives of our loved ones, especially Evan's, depended on it.

Chapter 2

The Program

℞ FOR STEPWIVES

PRESCRPTON

Directions: Apply all ten parts of following regimen daily, as needed:

P—Put the kids first.
R—Respect each other.
E—Empathize and acknowledge feelings.
S—Set limits and boundaries.
C—Claim your own baggage.
R—Remember realistic expectations.
P—Problem-solve.
T—Talk and communicate effectively.
O—Organize consistently.
N—Nurture yourself.

Contraindications: Above program is not intended to be used in conjunction with Egos. The use of "I" has been known to cause severe adverse reactions.

Marjorie Vega Krausz

Lynne Oxhorn-Ringwood

Louise Oxhorn

Ten long years of feuding had ended, and we had finally moved forward to become CoMamas. The heavy burden that weighed down our lives for so long had been lifted at last, and we found ourselves inspired to help other women benefit from the same sense of relief we were now experiencing. So we teamed up with Dr. Marjorie Krausz and developed our program.

Just as a doctor chooses a medication for treating an illness and writes a prescription, we have written a prescription to cure ailing stepwives. We use the acronym PRESCRPTON to identify our ten-step program. Each letter of the acronym represents one step in the program. You will notice, however, that the letter *I* is missing, meaning: Leave your "I's" (that is, your egos) behind when working the program. Easier said than done, we know.

Our PRESCRPTON program is no magic elixir. It is based on proven psychological and behavioral principles. But there is one catch: in order for the program to work, you must work it on a daily basis, just as you would any other lifestyle change, for example, dieting. And just like dieting, you won't see results overnight. You have to keep on working at it.

Now let's look at each step in detail.

P—*Put the Kids First*

The Wedding Present, by Louise:

> *Sometimes someone does something so seemingly out of character that it stops you in your tracks, which is exactly what happened to me when I opened Evan's wedding present. It didn't take a genius to figure out*

> that an eight-year-old boy couldn't have gone shopping on his own.
>
> As I stood holding the present Lynne had so generously taken Evan to get, I realized the real gift was the one Lynne had given her son: the one that allowed him to feel good about participating in his dad's wedding.

You are the adult, and the kids are who they're supposed to be: kids. As their mother, it is up to you to put your own personal feelings aside and consider what is best for your child. During and even after a divorce, your own emotional needs can be so great they can cloud your understanding of what is in your child's best interest. But their needs are the same as yours: to be loved and acknowledged, as well as to feel protected and secure. As the adult, it is up to you to fulfill these needs just as you would have had you stayed married.

As a stepmother, you must remain aware of the difficulties children face when their parent remarries and they have to adjust to a whole new family unit. No matter how happy you are to be part of this ready-made family, you must remember that the kids have suffered a loss.

When kids are not able or not permitted to verbalize their feelings, those feelings may manifest in a variety of problematic ways, such as stomachaches, headaches, whining, temper tantrums, withdrawal, or even extreme dependency behaviors. *Putting the kids first* means helping them to express their pent-up emotions, but you won't be able to do this unless you focus on what they, not you, are feeling.

Using the following techniques with your child can promote self-expression:

❧ The easiest way to find out how the kids are feeling is simply to ask.

❧ If they are too young or unable to verbalize, pay attention to how they react to particular situations or words.

❧ Drawing or participating in other forms of art often stimulates expression.

❧ Read age-appropriate books (see the Resources section at the end of this book) about blended families to them and discuss.

Putting the kids first does not mean giving in to their every whim or buying them the latest fads on the market. It means thinking of them before you think of yourself. It is essential to create a balanced, centered environment for the children, and although you may not always get what you want when you *Put the kids first,* the payoff will be healthy, happy children.

R—*Respect Each Other*

An incident from our cold war:

Evan was to receive a very prestigious award, and as usual, there were mixed feelings surrounding any event for him: sheer happiness at being able to share in the life of the child you love and utter despair because they would be there too. And as usual, things look a little different depending on where you're sitting.

Lynne:

The auditorium was almost full when Paul and I arrived. As we made our way toward the front, I saw an outstretched arm waving us down. It belonged to Louise. I sat down, happy to have such a seat for this proud occasion, yet knowing she hadn't really wanted to sit next to me any more than I wanted to sit next to her.

That day, to acknowledge their support, the parents were asked to stand up when their children were honored. Even I knew Louise had worked hard over the years helping Evan with his homework, driving him to school, and— I grudgingly had to admit—being a good stepmom to him. Somehow I felt a little sad when she just sat there after his name had been called, so I invited her to stand. She had earned the right to be recognized, too, whether I liked her or not.

Louise:

The auditorium was filling up quickly, and I figured I might as well save Lynne and Paul a seat. As they entered the room, I waved them over and waited apprehensively as they made their way toward us. As Lynne sat down next to me, I couldn't help but notice how very close the seats were—we were practically touching.

After what seemed like an eternity, Evan's name was called, and they asked that his parents stand up with him too. I sat quietly in my seat to allow Lynne the opportunity to bask in the glow of her son's glory, when she motioned for me to rise too. I was completely caught off guard: but happy. She had actually acknowledged me.

It was a rare moment indeed when we were able to show each other respect.

Respect, the foundation of any healthy relationship, means treating others as you would like to be treated. Respect comes in two varieties: self and shared. When you care enough about yourself to do the things you believe to be important, you are respecting yourself, and, contrary to what some may believe, taking care of yourself is *not* selfish. Getting along with others requires shared respect because even if you don't always agree with what the other person is saying, you can still respect her thoughts and feelings. Without these two components of respect, it is almost impossible to develop a healthy, working relationship.

When a marriage dissolves and a new marriage begins, both self and shared respect go out the window, and one's whole foundation seems to crumble. Is it any wonder that thinking clearly, working together, and problem solving seem like such impossible tasks? And herein lies the difficulty for stepwives: as the ex-wife, it is almost impossible to respect yourself when you hardly trust your own judgment anymore—after all, you thought your marriage would last forever. The idea of respecting your ex-husband, let alone his new wife, may seem absurd since you know next to nothing about her and may find his behavior questionable too. On the flip side, it can be difficult for the stepmother to respect the ex-wife when she has seen her dirty laundry or just doesn't agree with the parenting decisions she makes. And when she finds that perhaps new love isn't enough to make her live happily ever after as she once thought, self-doubts may plague her as well, leaving her to struggle with her own issues of self-respect.

If you continue finding yourself in situations where you end up feeling upset with yourself over your dealings with your stepwife, you need to work on improving your own self-respect. When we feel good about ourselves, it is easier to *respect each other.* Here's how to go about working on your own self-respect:

- List at least ten of the qualities you like about yourself. This list will represent your beliefs and values, and with this strong foundation clearly in mind, no one can change how you feel about yourself unless you let them.

- If you find yourself unable to come up with ten qualities you like about yourself, write down the qualities you would most like to incorporate into your life. To avoid becoming overwhelmed, tackle one at a time. The following are typical qualities and values you may want to consider:

Honesty: Do I share my feelings even when it's difficult?
Respect: Do I speak respectfully even when I'm angry?
Setting boundaries: Do I set appropriate boundaries to protect myself?
Nurture: Do I take care of myself emotionally, physically, and spiritually?
Self-confirmation: Do I believe in myself and know that I'm a good person?
Trust: Do I trust that I can problem-solve situations that come my way?

Consider the following questions as you work through your list:

Am I practicing my beliefs when I interact with my stepwife, ex, and children?
What can I do to improve my relationships and situation?

With your foundation and values clear, the process of respecting yourself can take place. With all the parents exhibiting respect toward one another, the children will have
not only one role model but several to teach them this very
important value. And remember that you don't have to like
each other to show respect.

E—*Empathize and Acknowledge Feelings*

> *Entry from the CoMamas guest book/Web site:*
>
> *I try not to let the things my husband's ex-wife says af-
> fect me. I wouldn't want to share my kids with another
> woman, so I try and empathize with what she must be
> going through. I even try and understand when she puts
> my husband down, which is not easy.*

Focusing only on your own feelings in the stepwife relationship will get you nowhere. It is so easy to feel angry with
her, but until you can take that next step and empathize
with how she may be feeling, you will continue to be en-
meshed in an ugly battle that will only keep escalating.
Of course, before you can begin to empathize with your
stepwife, you need to be able to identify and understand
your own feelings, and to do so, it is important to have an extensive "feeling vocabulary" as a means of expressing yourself. For instance, when stepwives tell us they feel out of

control, we ask them to zero in on what they are feeling and use more specific words such as *vulnerable, powerless,* or *afraid.* It is important to be specific and identify your feelings, because expressing your true feelings helps to resolve problems more quickly.

Building a feeling vocabulary takes practice. When you read the following list, check to see if you are stuck expressing only a few of the words in it. Remember, everyone's feelings are important, but the way we choose to deal with them is what creates a healthy or unhealthy relationship:

Sad
Angry
Lonely/need to be with someone
Alone/by myself in the world/I have no emotional support or understanding
Anxious
Out of control
Vulnerable
Happy
Worried
Fearful
Competitive
Revengeful
Frustrated
Relieved
Confused
Indifferent
Jealous
Hopeless
Insecure
Feelings of loss

Deal with the above words in this way:

✺ Choose the feelings you can identify with and try to come up with at least one reason for having each feeling.

✺ Try to avoid blaming anyone else for the way you are feeling.

✺ Think about situations or behaviors that have contributed to your feelings—for example, "I feel a sense of loss because I'm not the only mother figure to my child anymore" or "I feel insecure because I'm not always sure how to fulfill my role as stepmother."

Your relationship with your stepwife will begin to improve when you start to understand her feelings. Empathy disarms anger, especially in the stepwife arena, because it helps you see her as a human being rather than an enemy. Once you understand that her feelings are reasonable too, she will become an individual with an identity and not just a concept or an object to be hated.

The following exercise will help you develop empathy. Mentally switch places with your stepwife, and answer these questions as though you were she.

✺ What are your feelings about your role?

✺ What do you perceive your problems to be?

✺ How do these conflicts affect the children?

⬥ How does your stepwife communicate with you?

⬥ How does your stepwife treat you?

The purpose of empathizing is to put a problem in perspective by understanding the other person's point of view. Practicing empathy will pull you out of the emotional quicksand and allow you to become more objective.

Empathize and acknowledge feelings is perhaps the most formidable tool available to stepwives. Once you can understand exactly how you both are feeling, you will be able to take the first step toward becoming CoMamas.

S—*Set Limits and Boundaries*

The Soccer Mom, by Louise:

> Greg and I were going to Evan's soccer game, and never having been to a kid's soccer game before, I found myself just a little overdressed: I was wearing high heels!
>
> "I'm really sorry about your shoe," Greg said as we drove away after the game. Getting up from the wet grass after the game, my body stiff from sitting so long in such an unnatural position, I had stumbled, breaking the heel off my shoe.
>
> Weeks later, Greg and I attended a pregame meeting. "We're weeks into the season, and I still don't have a team mom," the coach grumbled. Not getting any response, he continued to look around the room, "Come on, people; I need a team mom. Anyone?"
>
> "Why don't you be team mom, Louise?" the other

*women urged. "M€?? I said, shocked, I don't think so."
"Oh, come on. It's no big deal, and the team could really
use you."*

*Feeling completely out of my element, I agreed any-
way. I did, after all, love €van, and if his team needed me,
how could I say no?*

The Soccer Mom, by Lynne:

*"Hi, it's Louise," she said perky as could be as I picked
up the phone. "I just wanted to let you know it's your turn
to bring snacks to €van's soccer game."*

*"Why are you the one assigning snacks?" I asked, con-
fused.*

*When she told me she would be team mom that season,
I felt my heart skip a beat. I couldn't understand how she
could possibly volunteer to be team mom for €van's soccer team without checking with me first. Didn't she get
it??? I'm €van's mom, not her. As I hung up the phone, I
couldn't help but wonder what her motives were. Was she
trying to take over my role as €van's mother?*

By definition, as stepwives, one of you has gone through
the trauma of divorce and the other has sort of taken over
her spot to become part of a preexisting—albeit defunct—
family. From where we're sitting, neither stepwife is in an
enviable position.

So how can two women peacefully coexist in a spot that is
really intended for only one? The key is to *set limits and
boundaries,* which will protect your rights not only as individuals but as two people who are part of the same family—
reluctant family members, as it were.

It is impossible to survive the stepwife relationship with your sanity intact unless you can *set limits and boundaries.* Boundaries help define who you are and separate "you" from "others." When you *set limits and boundaries,* you let your stepwife know how you feel and think and what actions you are expecting from her. If you accomplish this respectfully, there is little room for her to treat you in a controlling or manipulative manner, but remember the operative word: *respect.* Being angry or disrespectful when you speak with your stepwife implies that you don't really expect her to accept your limits. You have given away your power and can expect to begin feeling out of control.

If you fail to *set limits and boundaries,* you send the message that it is all right for her to continue her pattern of behavior. A classic example of boundary crossing in the stepwife arena is having your stepwife or ex-spouse come to your house unannounced. How can you let that person understand this behavior bothers you?

1. Analyze what bothers you about the situation.
2. Think about two options for improving it.
3. Tell your stepwife what behavior bothered you—in this case, "Yesterday you came to my house unannounced."
4. Offer a choice: "Would you prefer to meet in a neutral spot or call ahead so Tim can be waiting outside for you?"

It is important to understand the areas in which you need to set more limits. If you feel the need to speak up more, you have just acknowledged one area where you have the ability to set limits. Remember that you have the power to make decisions that will not only put the kids first, but will protect your right to have a separate and healthy life as well.

C—*Claim Your Own Baggage*

Louise's baggage:

> *I was my parents' midlife crisis: my father's little red sports car, my mother's premenopausal nightmare. My father was ecstatic, my mother less so, at the news of a baby on the way. My mother had been dreaming about her soon-to-be-empty nest, but it was not to be. Life threw her a curve ball in the form of another unexpected child— me. Her solution for dealing with "the situation" was to keep me out of her way. My earliest memory is of looking over the bars of my playpen awaiting the ride that would free me from my confinement and take me to nursery school. I was almost four years old.*
>
> *Is it any wonder that when I found myself in the role of stepmother, my presence clearly unwanted by Lynne, I felt four years old all over again, back in the playpen and completely controlled? And so I had to learn all over again how to stand up for myself.*

Lynne's baggage:

> *My parents had been childhood sweethearts, and their marriage after World War II was the topper to a perfect romance. When they discovered my mother was pregnant as planned, it was as if all their dreams had come true. As the first, I was loved and adored by my entire extended family, who welcomed me with open arms. Content with my idyllic life, I thought no one would ever take my place. But I can still remember the day my parents brought my*

> baby brother home from the hospital. As I watched them
> fussing over him, my eyes wide with hurt and disbelief, I
> felt that I had just been replaced.
>
> So years later, when Louise came on the scene, it felt
> like a reenactment of that painful time in my childhood,
> and all those old feelings came rushing back. This time, I
> felt even more jealous than I had when I was five.

Your baggage is your own personal history; your reaction
to all the behaviors, feelings, and messages you experienced
in childhood shapes you into who you are today. These reactions fall into patterns that dictate how we feel about ourselves, how we relate to others, and how we allow others to
relate to us. And whether you are an ex-wife or a stepmother,
you take your baggage with you wherever you go.

In order to begin healing the stepwife relationship, we
must not be afraid to look at how we are participating in
the conflict—in other words, *claim your own baggage.* Baggage comes in all shapes, sizes, and colors—some healthy,
some unhealthy. Since we are all imperfect (and we know all
you stepwives are thinking, *especially her*) we all have areas
in which we could improve.

When you *claim your own baggage,* you use your past as a
springboard for improving your future and empower yourself to change some of the thoughts, feelings, and perceptions that are standing in the way of your happiness and the
happiness of those around you. Looking at the past does not
have to mean hating one's parents for what they may have
done. It's an opportunity to sift through the many examples
you were exposed to as a child. Remember that parents do
the best they can based on what they themselves were
taught.

There are several questions we can ask ourselves to help isolate the issues we bring into the relationship that have nothing to do with our stepwife. Answering some of the questions may stir up emotions that may have been dormant for years, yet it is important to stay with these emotions until you can fully process them:

1. Identify your shortcomings or areas of insecurity (beauty or intellect, for example).
2. Look at your patterns of interaction in other relationships.
3. What are your hot buttons, and what types of personalities set you off most often?
4. How do you solve problems? Do you withdraw? Run away? Confront? Deny? Blame?
5. Have you ever responded to a person in your past the way you respond to your stepwife? How is she similar to that person? How is the situation similar?

Looking into your behavior, past and present, can create feelings of anxiety, anger, denial, and sadness. We know that staying with these feelings is often difficult, but if you are afraid to look into your history, you may never understand the patterns that molded you into who you are today. You will know you have successfully completed the process once you take ownership and no longer blame others (including your stepwife) for your reactions and responses.

When you explore your past and *claim your own baggage*, you can change the negative patterns that have been passed down to you through generations and actively ensure that they will not be passed on to your (step)children. The family you were born into has the most powerful and enduring influence on your life, but when you change the negative ways you deal with your past, you give your (step)children an opportunity to have the best conceivable baggage: healthy.

R—*Remember Realistic Expectations*

> *Lynne used to say to Louise, "What did you expect? You knew Greg had an ex-wife, and you knew it was me. You signed up for this."*
>
> *And Louise would reply: "What did you expect? You must have known that Greg would remarry and Evan would have a stepmother."*
>
> *The truth is that Lynne knew Greg would eventually remarry; she just thought he wouldn't do it until she was ready. And Louise thought being in love and marrying Greg would compensate for any problems that might crop up between her and Lynne. Needless to say, we both had very unrealistic expectations about being stepwives.*

All too often our expectations regarding relationships are influenced by our idealized notion of the way we think things should be, and the stepwife relationship is no exception. We have learned the hard way that expecting things to run smoothly in this arena is an error of colossal proportion. Believe it or not, to guarantee a healthier stepwife relationship, your best bet is to make it a point to expect things to go poorly much of the time. Expect divorce to be difficult. Expect being a stepmom to be complicated. Expect differences in parenting styles. That way, you won't be disappointed by the reality that will surely confront you.

What were you expecting your new life to be like? Ask yourself these questions:

~ Did you expect your ex-husband to remarry? If so, when?

~ Did you expect your ex-husband to be interested in your welfare after your divorce?

~ Did you expect his new wife to have an influence on his thinking?

~ Did you expect his children to like you immediately?

~ Did you expect his ex-wife to behave positively if he left her for you?

~ Did you expect his ex-wife to acknowledge you for helping with her children?

~ Did you expect to be in charge of financial decisions regarding his children?

Each time you find yourself becoming angry, ask yourself what you were expecting. Were your expectations reasonable? This reality check will help you deal with your anger when it comes up, and we assure you that it will. And if you constantly find that situations in the stepwife area are falling short of your expectations, it's time to develop and *remember realistic expectations.*

P—*Problem–Solve*

Since going into each other's houses was out of the question, we devised a drop-off/pick-up plan for getting Evan back and forth between houses. We always knew exactly the time Evan was to be dropped off or picked up.

> *When arriving to pick him up, we would simply honk the horn and patiently wait until he came out. When he was being dropped off, he would signal the person waiting in the car by flashing the porch light, letting the driver know that he had safely made it inside. Of course, for the plan to be successful, we had to be organized and give up all sense of spontaneity, but not having to see each other face to face made it more than worthwhile.*

With stepwives, the real problem is not whose fault it is, or what was done to whom, or why it happened. The real problem is that so few stepwives have effective strategies for solving the emotionally charged problems they face on a regular basis. But we have found that once stepwives learn and apply the basic principles of problem solving, they can successfully work out their own problems and keep themselves and their families out of court.

Our best advice is buy yourself some time. Rather than blowing up in anger when problems come up, use phrases like, "Let me think about that," or "I'll get back to you," until you feel capable of thinking in more practical terms. And once you actually begin to discuss the problem to be resolved, stay focused and avoid going off on emotional tangents. If things start heating up or getting off course, you can redirect by saying, "Let's get back to the main issue."

When your thinking is obscured by intense emotion, knowing how to use the following ten-step system to *problem-solve* will prove invaluable in untangling the conflict between stepwives:

1. Identify the problem you need to solve. (*Your stepwife or your ex has a key to the house.*)

2. Acknowledge feelings about the problem. (*It's my terri-tory now.*)
3. Claim your own baggage. (*I don't set limits*)
4. Empathize with your stepwife (*She misses her kids. Why would she want to live with my old stuff?*)
5. Gather information about the problem. (*Is anything out of the ordinary happening in my stepwife's life?*)
6. Come up with two options. (*Ask for the key back; change the locks*).
7. Did you put the kids first? (*If the answer is yes, then you are teaching them respect and the ability to set limits and boundaries.*)
8. Implement one option.
9. Evaluate the outcome.
10. If conflict still exists, try another solution.

Remember that effective problem solving is no guarantee that either stepwife will be happy with the outcome. Compromise is the name of the game in the stepwife arena: everybody gives up something. But when parents demonstrate the process of negotiation, resolution, and getting along with others, your children will benefit as they begin to learn the invaluable lessons of flexibility, tolerance, understanding, and respect for others.

T—*Talk and Communicate Effectively*

A CoMama subscriber wrote:

I am happily married to a man who has a daughter from his first marriage. She is having a lot of trouble fit-ting in at school. The real problem, though, is that her mother and I don't get along. I feel that I can't say any-thing without being criticized, and I'm afraid she's go-ing to try and take my stepdaughter away. It's gotten so bad that I can't even hear her name without getting upset.

Stating what you think and feel in a direct yet respectful manner can be an arduous task, especially if you're em-broiled in a volatile situation like the one with your step-wife. When you are agitated, it is not only difficult to understand your own feelings; it can become almost impos-sible to express yourself properly. By using some of the com-munication techniques we mention, you will learn how to share your true feelings and thoughts and work toward re-solving your problems and conflict with your stepwife.

"I" statements are one of the most powerful tools you can use when communicating with your stepwife and (ex)spouse. We've all experienced someone's saying, "You made me feel___." This kind of statement automatically puts one on the defensive and takes the attention away from the problem you are trying to resolve. It's easier to solve problems when you can focus on a specific issue. Use this format: "I [state feeling] when I [see, hear] you [describe be-havior]"—for example, "I felt so angry when I heard you bad-mouthed me to the children."

Reflective listening is similar to looking in a mirror and describing what you see. You reflect another person's feel-ings by restating the same emotions or meaning she has ex-pressed to you. Showing that you respect the other person's feelings will help you gain her cooperation in solving a problem. For example, if she said, "We waited for over twenty minutes for you to pick Lily up. That makes me really mad," the reflective response would be, "I understand you and Lily were very upset that I didn't get here on time."

Finally, *clarification* is used to make sure everyone is actually talking about the same issues and understanding each other's words. To clarify, you can either ask a question or restate the information you just heard. For example, if she says, "Why do you keep calling all the time? We're too busy to talk all the time," the clarification response would be, "Are you saying you would like me to call less or not at all?"

When you have the patience and skill to listen to each other, you will be able to relate more effectively, reach a compromise, and negotiate a solution to the problems you are facing. If you do not hear what the other person is saying, you will be a contributing factor in the resulting miscommunication. So no matter which technique you choose, the important thing is to *talk and communicate effectively.*

O—*Organize Consistently*

Evan was king at both our houses, and because we shared custody, no one got to see him all the time. When we did see him, we cherished that time all the more, making discipline a very difficult chore.

Like most other kids, Evan would find himself in trouble from time to time. If he did something during Louise and Greg's time, by the time he returned to Lynne's, it was already old news. So we decided that wherever Evan was, the consequences of his behavior followed him. That way no one was the heavy.

Evan told us years later that having the same rules made living in two houses a lot easier for him.

Imagine what it would be like to live in two separate houses—living out of a suitcase, separated from those you love, your friends never knowing where they can reach you. The mere idea of going back and forth without a permanent place to live would be more than we, as adults, could ever possibly cope with.

Divorce exerts cataclysmic changes in a child's life. When children are forced to live in two different homes with two different sets of rules to follow, complications multiply. But when there is a plan to *organize consistently*, it becomes possible for children to develop a sense of security and trust. And although it seems logical, it bears saying that what is most important when you *organize consistently* is to do so in a healthy, productive way rather than a negative or defeating manner.

The process of being consistent involves talking and communicating effectively, developing good problem-solving skills, and ensuring cooperation among all the parents. *Organizing consistently* is essential in the following areas:

- Health care

- Discipline

- House rules

- Chores

- Bedtime

- School and homework

- Sports

- Holidays

- Child care

When all the parents are united by having similar rules and expectations, the children will feel like they have many parents who love and respect them, rather than two separate households of people competing for their love and attention.

N—*Nurture Yourself*

Entry from the CoMamas guest book/Web site:

Whatever you do, don't let his ex get to you. Instead, smile every time you see her, and work on making yourself feel better. What works for me is setting aside some time just for me to do something I really like. When I feel better, it seems that I can cope with her a little easier.

The stepwife relationship is a difficult one at best, and because it's difficult, it is doubly important that you *nurture yourself.* That includes your mental, emotional, physical, and spiritual self. Feeling angry, frustrated, or even sorry for yourself will not change the reality of your situation. If you *nurture yourself,* you will be in a much better position to accept your life and take care of those around you, especially your children.

We know how hard it can be to treat yourself well, so here are some suggestions to get you started:

- ❧ Take a healthy escape. Go for a walk, call a friend, or find a quiet place to just be.

- ❧ Pamper yourself. Get a massage, have your nails or hair done (get together with a friend and do each other's hair and nails), take a long, hot bubble bath, or read a book.

- ❧ Center yourself. Meditate, practice yoga, dance, exercise, or keep a journal.

- ❧ Fortify yourself. Start a hobby, take a class, get involved in the arts, or learn something new.

Energizing yourself and renewing your strength and endurance is necessary for working on the stepwife relationship. Once you feel better about yourself, you may just start to feel better about the predicament you're in.

The ten steps of the PRESCRPTON do not have to be used collectively, but that doesn't mean you won't find yourself in a situation where you will need to use all ten steps. Every chapter demonstrates how the PRESCRPTON works by presenting common problems stepwives face and showing how steps from the PRESCRPTON can be used. We recommend that if you get stuck, refer back to this chapter for the details on how to apply each step.

When we tell other stepwives about our getting together, we often hear things like, "Well, that was all fine for you, but my stepwife would never even think of talking to me," or "Are you kidding? You two were lucky; you were both reasonable. But there's nothing I can do if my stepwife won't cooperate." But now there is something you can do: you can begin using the PRESCRPTON even if you have to do it by yourself. Becoming CoMamas can't be hurried along; it is a process that takes time and patience. But the fact is that two out of every three second marriages fail, and most succumb to divorce due to the hardships inherent in the extended-blended family. Let us help you and your children avoid becoming just another statistic.

Chapter 3

Wicked or Wonderful? What Kind of Stepmother Are You?

From Louise's journal:

> *10/08/87   It's 3:00 A.M., and I'm way too excited to sleep—tonight I met the man I'm going to marry! When I opened the door and saw Greg standing there, time stood still—we were instantly connected by some powerful force greater than we were.*
>
> *11/17/87   Things just keep getting better and better—if that's possible. It's like we knew each other the moment we met. And I just want to sing and dance and shout from the rooftops—we're in love, we're in love, we're in love.*
>
> *8/23/88   We fit so well into each other's lives. Everyone thinks we are just the best thing that ever happened to each other. And Evan, his Evan, is the cutest little boy. Sometimes he's just waiting for me to come over so we can play Lincoln Logs or G.I. Joe—imagine me playing games with a little boy and loving every minute of it. Life couldn't be better—except of course for Lynne. I can hardly stand to say her name. But no matter, I'm going to be the best stepmother ever.*

Why is it that when people hear the word *stepmother*, they automatically think "wicked"? As the ex-wife, you're probably thinking she's earned every syllable of that title she's been carrying for so long. She's wheedled her way into your ex-husband's life and convinced him that the two of you were "never a match." And now she's gotten him to believe that she loves your kids like you do. Why can't she just leave your past alone? And what gives *her* the right to criticize your every move?

Contrary to popular opinion among ex-wives, most stepmothers are not wicked. Unlike many first wives, stepmothers never get the chance to form an exclusive bond with their new husbands. They've married a man with children and live in the ex-wife's shadow, often subjected to criticism from the children and other family members. And most are ill equipped to handle the wrath they may encounter from the ex-wife. Given the circumstances, who wouldn't be wicked?

Stepmother Defined

The notion of what a stepmother is has changed over the years. Many experts in this field have challenged the idea that the stepfamily is defined by marriage. As stated in the *Los Angeles Times,* less than one-fourth of all households in this country contain a married couple and their children, and the number of unmarried couples living together has increased astronomically. Almost 40 percent of couples living together without the sanctity of marriage live with children not necessarily their own. We acknowledge all types of stepfamilies regardless of their legal status.

What Makes Me a Wicked Stepmother?

Sometimes stepmothers are unaware of how their behavior affects their stepwife:

> *I loved Evan. He was so cute and affectionate, always hugging and kissing me as if it were the most natural thing in the world. I couldn't understand why Lynne seemed so upset the time she witnessed this behavior. Wasn't she happy I loved her child?*

Louise felt that diving right into her role as stepmother was precisely what would make her "wonderful." In Lynne's eyes, however, this made her a "wicked" stepmother—someone who crossed her boundaries and was therefore dangerous and out of control. Just like Louise, most stepmothers wonder when they will be acknowledged for their willingness to devote themselves to their stepchildren. They often realize, too late, that their stepwife has condemned them for assuming their new role too quickly and too ardently. Herein lies the stepwife paradox.

Because most stepmothers are well meaning and want to be considered wonderful, we have included the following questions as a way to help you assess your behavior and determine whether you are overstepping your stepwife's boundaries as mother:

ᴥ *Do you volunteer to participate in events in the children's lives, such as room mom or team mom, without consulting their mother?* Even if your stepchildren ask you to participate, even if your husband encourages your participation, do not become involved unless you check with their mother first. It's never too late to set this rule, and it will pay off quickly. By respecting her boundaries in this way, you will gain her trust, and eventually she may be able to relax her vigilance.

◆§ *Are you rude to the children's mother when she calls your house?* If you have trouble speaking civilly to your stepwife on the phone, try this technique: Rehearse what you will say when you pick up the phone and find her on the other end. Try something simple like, "Sure, hang on" or "I'll get him for you" when she asks to speak to someone in your home. Being prepared in this way gives you the opportunity to avoid potential problems by treating her in a civilized manner—respecting her rather than being rude to her.

◆§ *Do you hover over your husband while he's on the phone with your stepwife?* Although it's very tempting to coach your husband from the sidelines, this will only upset the balance of this already precarious situation and you will be the one to suffer when you find that your relationship has become all about her. Permit them the courtesy to speak about their children privately. And if you find yourself falling into the almost unavoidable trap of grilling your husband about their conversations, remove yourself from the room and find something else to occupy your time. Your household will be much more peaceful and harmonious if you can do this.

◆§ *Do you give your stepwife advice about her children before she asks for it? Don't!* Would you give your children's teacher advice on how to teach, even if you were a teacher? Of course not. Extend this same courtesy to your stepwife.

◆§ *Are you openly affectionate with the children in the mother's presence?* This behavior, although well intentioned, is very upsetting to the mother. If you know your stepwife is coming to pick up the kids, empathize with how she may be feeling and say your good-bys before she arrives. If you happen to run into your stepchildren in public with their mother, try greeting them with a smile and a big hello—some small gesture that respects everyone's boundaries.

If you've answered yes to any of these questions, it might be time to Claim Your Own Baggage. You may have to take some of the responsibility for the problems you are having with your stepwife. Remind yourself that you are the stepmother, not the natural mother, and no matter the circumstances surrounding your entrance into your new family, you are the one who must adjust your behavior and demeanor to fit into this preexisting family unit.

Here are typical emotions of a stepmother. Have you ever felt like this?

Discounted	Confused	Frustrated
Unappreciated	Angry	Energized
Controlled	Slighted	Hated
Resentful	Powerless	Misunderstood
Unwanted	Jealous	Insulted

If you've ever endured any of these feelings, you are not alone: most stepmothers feel all this and more. By increasing your feeling vocabulary, you will become more comfortable in expressing yourself.

A Rose by Any Other Name

> **A CoMama subscriber wrote:**
>
> When I was little, my parents got divorced, and my dad remarried. My dad and his new wife made me call her mom, and I hated it. I've just married a man with children, and I will never make them call me mom. It's just not right.

We often have stepmothers tell us that their stepchildren call them mom. To say this is extremely upsetting to the ex-wife is an understatement. Mothers will indeed feel you are wicked if you allow your stepchildren to call you mom. Instead, we suggest you and your stepchildren come up with a special name you all feel comfortable with. Here are examples of what some of the people we've heard from call themselves:

- ❧ Noni, Omi ("other mother")

- ❧ *Mother* in another language—for example, *ima* (Hebrew) *madre* (Spanish)

- ❧ S'mom (stepmom)

- ❧ A derivative of the stepmom's name, which is what Louise did:

> For as long as I can remember, Evan has called me Weese. As a kid, I never liked that nickname. Somehow,

> *though, when Evan said it, it sounded so endearing that I actually began to prefer it to Louise. Now even my friends call me Weese.*

You don't need to be called mom to feel special and appreciated by your stepchildren. Their mother has every right to oppose her kids calling another woman by the name reserved for the one and only person who is truly mom. Even if your stepchildren want to call you mom, do not encourage this. This will only confuse them and create enormous hostility between you and their mother. As a stepmother, you need to cultivate a relationship with the children that does not diminish the relationship they have with their mother. No matter how much they love you and you love them, you are *not* their mother. She has already had to give up a tremendous amount. Do not make this very precarious situation worse by having her children call you mom. Leave her with that. It is the least she deserves.

What Kind of Stepmother Are You?

Our research has uncovered several types of stepmothers, each of whom poses a threat to the ex-wife:

- The Wendy

- The Mother Wendy

- The Looking-for-a-Daddy-for-My-Kids

- The I'll-Be-a-Better-Mother-the-Second-Time-Around

❧ The Yours, Mine, and Ours

❧ The Heroine

Decide which one you or your stepwife may be. By understanding why a stepmother does the things she does, you will be taking the first step toward improving your situation.

The Wendy

Louise was a Wendy. The Wendy takes us back to the classic tale of Peter Pan and that marvelous character, Wendy, who cared for the motherless children in Never Never Land. The Wendy may or may not have been married before, but she does not have children of her own. She is very excited to rush to the aid of the "motherless" children who have become part of her ready-made family.

If you are a Wendy, you may feel that since his ex-wife did not do her job well enough to keep her family together, the opportunity is now yours to fill the void in the lives of these children. You may feel sorry for their poor father, who has had to adjust to being Mr. Mom. And so, like Louise, you dedicate your life to making their lives better:

> *Greg and Evan. If you say it fast, it's almost like saying one name. They were so cute together. They reminded me of the characters on that old TV show,* The Courtship of Eddie's Father. *But something was missing from their lives, and I was pretty sure I knew what that something was: me. It was almost as if I had been sent to them to make their family complete.*

The Wendy is particularly difficult for the ex-wife to deal with. She can go through all the motions of being a mother, yet does not seem to understand the innermost feelings of a biological mother. The amount of energy and zeal the Wendy focuses on her "new children" may send the ex-wife into fits of anger stemming from the fear that her children will love their "new" mother more than their "old" one.

Ex-wives:

❧ This is a good time to kill her with kindness. Call your stepwife, and share your fears about her becoming more important to your children than you are. Allow her to understand just how vulnerable you are feeling. By communicating in this way, she will be able to empathize with you and, you hope, want to adjust her behavior accordingly.

Stepmothers:

❧ As excited as you are, tread lightly. Allow everyone time to adapt to your presence in their lives. Remember that only your husband invited you to this party. Of course, you will never feel that you are entering your new life quickly enough, and your stepwife will always feel you are coming in too quickly. Such is the nature of the stepwife relationship: no one gets exactly what they want.

❧ Are you intentionally overlooking your stepwife because it would be so much easier if it were you, your husband, and his kids? If you are, it's time to claim your own baggage and get started on changing your attitude.

The Mother Wendy

A participant at one of our workshops shared this:

I really wanted kids, so Bruce agreed to reverse his vasectomy. I was so thrilled when I found out I was pregnant. His ex, on the other hand, wouldn't even acknowledge our happiness, and I was worried she would say mean things about the baby to her children.

The only thing worse than a Wendy to an ex-wife is a pregnant Wendy: a soon-to-be Mother Wendy. There are four words that strike terror in the heart of every ex-wife: *We're having a baby.* Now the ex-wife is consumed with visions of her kids being cast into a dark cellar with no food or water, like the children in an old fairy tale, or at the very least, playing second fiddle to the stepmother's child. But the Mother Wendy is afraid too. She fears her husband will love his other kids more than her child. Where will her baby fit in? Whose child will be daddy's little boy or girl?

Lynne recollects:

When I heard Greg and Louise were planning to have a child of their own, I guess those old childhood fears of being replaced came flooding back. I was terrified that if Louise had a child of her own, Evan would become the forgotten stepchild. I wrote a long letter begging them not to. Before I sent it, I ran it by a friend of mine, a younger second wife, who discouraged me from sending it. But I couldn't keep myself from at least making a phone call to plead my case. I felt my child's welfare was at stake.

Stepwives:

- Since you are both experiencing similar feelings—already walking in each other's shoes—now is a very good time for you to claim your own baggage by sharing your fears with your stepwife. Initiating this conversation during the pregnancy will help smooth out the transition that will occur when the baby actually arrives. And, remember, it doesn't matter who brings the issue up as long as one of you is brave enough to put it on the table.

- Institute a plan to *organize consistently.* This will help the children with the uncertainty they may feel regarding their differing custody arrangements. Because your stepchildren will be rotating in and out of your house, while your child has only one home, post a large family calendar to keep track of each of their schedules, using a different color for each child. This will provide them all with a sense of structure and security, and everyone will know who will be where and when.

If stepwives are feeling insecure about the changes the new baby will bring, imagine what the emotions of the existing children are like.

The Looking-for-a-Daddy-for-My-Kids

Janice didn't know how she was going to make it on her own with four kids. When she met A.J., she felt it was the answer to her prayers. She would have a man again, and her kids would have a father.

Although your children probably have a daddy of their own and may even see him regularly, wouldn't it be nice to have a man around the house? Think of the trash, homework, and tax return time, not to mention that big empty bed of yours. The Looking-for-a-Daddy-for-My-Kids hopes blending her family with that of a man who has children will make her life ideal, kind of like the Brady Bunch. (Of course, the Bradys didn't have to deal with exes. Theirs were dead.)

In this situation, the ex-wife is afraid the stepmom's household, with its new brothers and sisters, will be more fun than her house. What if her kids have so much fun there they never want to come home to her? The ex-wife may also be concerned that you are not treating her children as well as you are treating your own. In fact, this same feeling is sure to arise in your new husband and in your stepchildren alike, so you need to remain constantly aware of dealing with everyone fairly. Conversely, you may feel your new husband favors his own children over your kids. By *talking and communicating effectively,* you can address everyone's concerns before they develop into full-blown resentments.

Unlike the Brady Bunch, every blended family does not come with three boys and three girls conveniently spaced and able to get along famously. Most have lots of problems, including having to deal with two mothers.

Stepmothers:

◆ Show you're a team player, and alleviate your stepwife's concerns by calling and asking her the following questions: "Is there anything you'd like me to know about ___ when he's with me? Is there anything you'd like me to do or not do when he's with me?" Let her know you do not want to be the child's mother; you just want to provide a safe, secure home for her kids when they are with you.

Ex-wives:

- ✿ Talk to your kids, and share with them how happy you are that they're having fun at their dad's and stepmom's, *even if it kills you.* By *putting the kids first* in this way, you will allow them to feel comfortable when they are with their father and stepmother—something every child has a right to.

- ✿ No matter how overwhelmed you may be feeling, don't forget to participate in activities with your children while they are with you. Take a nature walk, go to the park or beach, play a game, or read together, making life with you fun too.

The I'll-Be-a-Better-Mother-the-Second-Time-Around

Sue posted the following on our website bulletin board:

People often think my daughter and I are sisters. I had her when I was eighteen, and we grew up together. I made so many mistakes along the way, sometimes it was hard to tell who was the mother and who was the child. Now she's twenty-five, and I'm ready to start all over again.

If this sounds a little like your life, you may be what we call an I'll-Be-a-Better-Mother-the-Second-Time-Around.

You said good-bye to "happily ever after," and with that, gave up all hope of ever finding love again. When you discover yourself falling head over heels not only with a new man but with his children as well, it's as though you've been given a second chance at love *and* motherhood. And if your life as a single mom was a struggle, you probably learned a thing or two about being a mom along the way. Of course, you want to share your hard-earned wisdom with your new family.

As an I'll-Be-a-Better-Mother-the-Second-Time-Around, maybe it's been a while since you've been an active parent. You may have forgotten how it feels to be an ex-wife or single mom. You probably need some reminding if you catch yourself questioning your stepwife's parenting skills, becoming upset when she speaks to your husband about their children, or resenting spousal or child support payments. To counteract any of these *very normal* feelings, we suggest you take a trip back in time.

Stepmothers:

&s Remember how you felt when you were in her shoes. Empathize and acknowledge feelings she may be having. Ask yourself if, when you were a single mom, all of *your* parenting decisions were sound. Did you ever need to speak to your children's father about important issues? Remember your own financial arrangements. Did you receive spousal or child support? If not, would you have been better off if you had? Recall the time you are so happy to have left behind. Equipped with this information, you will have a bet-ter chance of understanding and respecting your stepwife's role as mother, even though you may not like her.

Ex-wives:

- ❧ Be happy that the woman entering your children's life has the experience of being a mom already. Although she may seem overly enthusiastic or even critical of you at times, your children will benefit from her time, attention, and previous "on-the-job training."

- ❧ To break the ice and get to know each other, ask her about her experiences as a mother. Try relating to her woman to woman or mother to mother. Although her children are grown, you may find that your kids may relate to her kids as role models or even mentors— one more plus for your kids.

Yours, Mine, and Ours

Tamara had been a single mom for five years. At age thirty-eight, she not only wanted to get married again, but, certain her biological clock was running out, she was desperate for another child. When she married Koby, she was excited about blending their families and ecstatic over the prospect of creating a child together.

The perfect ending to a perfect story. You've met the man of your dreams—again. Your children and his children are brothers and sisters, and now you are having a baby together. What could possibly be better?

It is important to recognize that just as in the Mother Wendy scenario, the children are probably feeling vulnerable about the arrival of the new baby. There are things that you can do to help solve some of the inherent problems you will face surrounding the birth of this baby.

Stepmothers:

& You can help your stepchildren feel wanted by giving each child an opportunity to share in the excitement taking place, such as helping name the baby or going to the doctor's appointments.

& Once the baby arrives, let each child participate by allowing them to help care for the baby, while being careful not to overburden them with too much responsibility. This will help them feel they are still important members of the family.

& To ensure that everyone feels recognized, do something commemorative for all the children in your newly blended family, such as putting together a personal scrapbook or special photo album.

Ex-wives:

& You have the capacity, as well as the responsibility, to help your children adjust to the enormous changes taking place in their new family. Like it or not, this baby is coming, and the way you handle it with your children will influence the effect it has on them.

& Act happy for them, telling them how much fun having a new brother or sister will be. After the big event, ask questions about the baby's progress. Take your children shopping for a present for the baby, letting them know it's all right to feel excited about their new sibling.

❧ Be sure to spend some extra time with each of your children, answering any questions they might have or engaging in an activity they particularly enjoy.

❧ In case the children are not happy about having a new sibling, give them the opportunity to discuss their feelings. Address their fears of being replaced by reassuring them that they will continue to have an important role.

The Heroine

Sharyn at a women's wellness convention:

My husband's ex-wife has been in and out of jail for the past ten years for drug abuse. We got married seven years ago, and since then, I have been mother to his three kids. Every time she gets out of jail, the courts give her supervised visits to our house. She always shows up late and leaves early. She's ruining those kid's lives, and there is nothing I can do about it.

Unfortunately, we hear from a growing number of Heroine stepmothers who have assumed almost total responsibility for raising their stepwife's children. Although this type of stepmom may also fall into one of the other stepmother categories, her role as the Heroine dominates her experience as a stepmom.

The Heroine often feels like the hired help. She works hard to take care of her stepchildren while their own mother is free to do as she pleases. Resentment runs rampant, whether the ex-wife is off taking drugs, having an affair, or pursuing a career. There is a plus side to this problem, however: the stepmother usually has little interference from her absentee stepwife and does not have to contend with conflict on a regular basis. Still, when the ex-wife does become involved, the problems may be even more disruptive to the status quo the Heroine has established but does not have complete control over. Her life has been completely changed by her stepwife's reappearance, and it will be almost impossible for her to Put the Kids First if she continually feels resentful.

Stepmothers:

❧ Do not hesitate to nurture yourself in this situation. If you don't do it, no one else will do it for you. Engage your husband's cooperation by explaining that if you do not take care of yourself, you will be unable to take care of his children properly. We assure you there is nothing selfish about this.

❧ Make a list of the things that replenish you and do them. Here are some examples in a variety of nurturing categories:

Physical	Emotional	Spiritual	Intellectual	Sensual
Walk	Journal	Worship	Take a class	Music
Dance	See friends	Books	History Channel	Romantic meal
Nap	Movie	Mountains	Museum	Bubble bath

By picking from all five categories regularly, it will be possible to keep yourself from resenting the care you are giving to the others in your household.

Wicked or Wonderful?

Once you have determined the kind of stepmother you are, take this quiz to find out if you conform to the fairy tales and are indeed a wicked stepmother or whether you have surpassed this image to become a wonderful stepmother.

Quiz

1. When your stepchildren are present, you:
   a. hide your negative feelings about their mother.
   b. speak your true thoughts.
   c. cast a spell over their mother as you stir your cauldron.
2. When your stepchild needs to be disciplined, you:
   a. discuss disciplinary actions with his or her father.
   b. tell the child's mother, and let *her* worry about her own brats.
   c. turn the child to stone.
3. When your stepchildren have a role in a school performance, you:
   a. willingly attend.
   b. decide you need to wash your hair that night.
   c. fly away on your broom.

Scoring: If you chose *a* for every answer, congratulate yourself. You are a wonderful stepmother. If you chose *b* for every answer, consider yourself a stepmother who is still learning on the job. You need to continue developing your skills, and work toward the goal of *putting the kids first.* If you chose *c* for every answer, you may have already guessed: you are a classic wicked stepmother. Get some help right away!

From Wonderful to Wicked—and Back Again

The behaviors and situations in the list that follow have been described to us over and over again by women all over the world. They are potential land mines. The list highlights the most common issues we hear about and will expand on in later chapters. Pay attention to them, because they may threaten your ability to be the wonderful stepmother you hope to be:

- Your stepwife's behavior is controlling.

- Your stepwife is constantly bad-mouthing you.

- Your stepwife is still dependent on your husband.

- Your stepwife does not acknowledge you.

- Your stepchildren may not like you, and you may not like them.

- Your husband may not allow you to discipline his children.

- You may resent the financial arrangements between your husband and stepwife.

- Your in-laws may prefer your stepwife.

When you *remember realistic expectations* of what your new life could be like, you may be able to deal with these possibilities before they become realities.

Commonly Asked Questions

The fact that stepmothers have been around since the beginning of time speaks to their importance. As a stepmother having undertaken the huge responsibility of mothering someone else's children, you need to think of yourself not as another mother but as a member of the parenting team. The following are the most commonly asked questions from stepmothers:

Why doesn't my stepwife want to meet me? Your stepwife is not in any hurry to meet you because she does not want you in her life. When you question her sense of responsibility as a mother just because she doesn't want to meet the woman who will be playing such a big part in her children's lives, she feels judged and criticized and may react with a vicious outpouring of emotion. It's really difficult to grasp how the ex-wife is feeling, especially if you aren't a mother yourself. And unless your stepwife is willing to acknowledge her vulnerability and take a risk in meeting early on, you can be sure that misunderstandings and poor communication will develop into a vast array of problems.

What does my stepwife have against me? I didn't break up her marriage. Here's what the stepmother needs to realize: to share one's child with another woman goes against every fiber in a mother's being. Primal responses are set off, and once triggered, they are difficult to contain. Understanding what's at the core of the ex-wife's behavior will help you see why she behaves the way she does. It is difficult for the stepmother to comprehend this because the stepmother and the ex-wife are on completely different emotional levels when it comes to the children. The stepmother cares for the children, but she sees them more from a practical than emotional standpoint, especially early on.

Why won't she acknowledge me? It's the stepmother's presence alone that can ignite deep-seated feelings of powerlessness within the ex-wife over not being able to be a full-time mother. The ex-wife feels as if she's been demoted as she perceives her ex-husband pulling her children out of her arms and placing them into the arms of this other woman— the woman he has chosen to promote to (step)mother. The ex-wife feels the stepmother is already receiving more than enough acknowledgment from her ex. Why should she give her more? Instead, it's more satisfying to knock her down a few notches.

Do not be disheartened by what you may encounter along the way as you settle into your role of stepmother. Knowing what to expect will ensure your ability to become, and remain, a wonderful stepmother in the eyes of your stepchildren and in the eyes of your stepwife. By adhering to the PRESCRPTON, you will have the power to control your own future.

Chapter 4

The Princess Bride Ex-Wife and Others

> Dear Greg,
>
> Here I am, alone and writhing in pain on our first Christmas apart. And as I lie here, overcome with an overwhelming anguish that causes my body to ache and tremble inside, I am seized with visions of you and Evan joyfully unwrapping presents with her.
>
> You have always been my strength, my security, and my safe haven—the one I depended on when times got tough. But now, at the most difficult point in my life, I have been shut out, and someone else has taken my place. Why did I ever let you go?

If you are divorced, you know that whether your marriage was long or short, passionate or polite, close or distant, its end signaled the loss of your entire way of life. It was the loss of your primary relationship and most likely created a gigantic hole where there once was a full life.

As a stepmother, you may be asking yourself if you should care about the pain of an ex-wife who can be nasty and controlling. The answer is yes! She's in your life, like it or not. It is precisely the fact that ex-wives feel so completely out of control that causes them to try to control those around them. It will be a lot easier if you understand what motivates her to behave the way she does. As the ex-wife, you probably think you already know what your motivations are, but perhaps we can give you additional insight. We have learned that while you are drowning in a world of pain and confusion, your behavior will have a direct effect on your children. What you do and say during this very critical time will set the tone for how your children will develop—healthy and balanced or hostile and confused.

The Grief Cycle

Divorce triggers all the same feelings as the death of a loved one. As soon as your marriage is over, you will most likely plunge into what psychologists refer to as the grief cycle, identified by Elisabeth Kübler-Ross. The grief cycle is a chain of feelings usually experienced after a significant loss of any kind. Following is a modified version of Kübler-Ross's model:

- Shock

- Denial

- Anger

- Depression

- Acknowledgment

- Acceptance

This is not an overnight process; it can take years for a woman to work through these devastating feelings and finally come out on the other side. It has been said that the length of the entire grief process in a divorce is equal to half the length of the marriage. You could be anywhere in the process when your ex-spouse begins to date and ultimately remarry, and he won't usually check with you to see if you're ready for it. It's a cruel quirk of nature, but men typically become involved in new relationships and remarry more often and more quickly than women, so it is quite common for an ex-wife still to be grieving when that new woman is introduced. And when she makes her entrance, whether you are at the beginning or the end of the cycle, get ready to be thrust once again into that abyss of churning emotions. Even if you are no longer in love with your ex-husband, the grief over the loss of your main role as "the only mother in your child's life" will be enough to reignite all of those old reactions. The good news is, however, that the further into the grief cycle you are, the more effective you will be in working through it the second time around.

Let's take a look at the sequence of feelings you will, or may have already encountered, as unpleasant as they are, as the stepmother becomes more firmly entrenched in your life:

- Shock. You have been dethroned. You are now expected to have a relationship with a woman you had no control in choosing. Not only will you have to relate to her, but your child is being exposed to her as well. Your guard is up.

- Denial. You absolutely can't believe anyone could ever take *your* place; you and your husband were made for each other. Of course, when he learns more about her, he'll decide that she could never compare to you and will want to come back to you so you can be one big, happy family again. (Not!)

❧ Anger. You begin hearing more about their love and all the fun they're having with *your* child, and you become angrier. You've just bought your ticket for a roller-coaster ride of emotions: feeling angry, alone, curious, depressed, numb, confused, and then angry all over again. You are in the primal mode, and all of your mothering instincts have been aroused. And the more out of control you feel, the more you begin making demands on your ex-husband and the stepmother. How dare *anyone* mess with your right to be the one and only mother to the child you bore?

❧ Depression. You are alone, and no one cares what you are going through. Your friends have started socializing with your ex-husband and his wife. You feel as if you've been abandoned and that everything is crashing down around you. You are in pain, and it is impossible to believe that it will ever go away.

❧ Acknowledgment. You begin to realize that this has become your reality, and as much as you hate it, there's nothing you can do to change it. You are divorced, your ex-husband has remarried, your child has a stepmother, and his family and your mutual friends have accepted her. It's over.

❧ Acceptance. You begin to make new friends, resume dating, and move forward in your life, looking toward the future rather than trying to hang on to the past. As you progress through acceptance, your self-esteem blossoms, and you find yourself feeling proud of yourself and your accomplishments. It becomes easier to live with the fact that your child has a stepmother. You stop cringing at the mere mention of her name. You have accepted your new life.

This grieving cycle can be long and arduous, but there are some things you can do to ease the process:

- Recognize you are going to go through this process. Acknowledge your feelings, and get a good sense of how far along you are in it. Often, just *remembering realistic expectations* and allowing yourself to feel these emotions will help you get through it faster.

- Decide you've spent enough energy on grieving and move on. Nurture yourself by figuring out what you want more of in your life, and go after it. You cannot control his relationship with the new woman in *his* life, but you can control the other aspects of *your* life.

- Acknowledge that your ex-spouse and his wife will have a relationship in spite of your feelings.

Why It's Easier to Be a Grieving Widow Than an Ex-Wife

A widowed woman is expected to grieve. In fact, those two words—*grieving* and *widow*—often go hand in hand. The grieving widow engenders sympathy from all. She is never shunned, but looked on as someone who has lost not only her life companion, but also the father of her children, her breadwinner, her "hero," her protector, and, most of all, her way of life. No one would ever dream of turning against a widow in her time of need. She is seen as a victim, as someone to whom life has dealt a terrible blow. For her considerable losses, she receives universal solace: sympathy cards, kind neighbors who bring casseroles, and in many cases, an insurance company that will present her with some kind of death benefit. She has lost her husband, but has been scooped up into the bosom of her friends, family, and community.

When a woman divorces, she too has lost her life companion, the father of her children, her breadwinner, her "hero," her protector, and her way of life. To this we must add that her husband, whom she may still be in love with, will usually remarry or be living with someone else soon after the separation, forcing her to endure the pain of rejection as well. She does not receive sympathy cards or casseroles, even if he left her for a younger woman, and no insurance benefit automatically comes to her. In fact, many women don't even receive spousal or child support, and if they do, usually, it's not without a legal battle that she may have to pay for. And when she continues to grieve, exasperated friends and family often tell her, "Get over it!" Is it any wonder she feels abused, abandoned, and betrayed?

Here are typical emotions of an ex-wife: Have you ever felt like this?

Betrayed	Replaced	Threatened
Discarded	Shunned	Powerless
Vulnerable	Jealous	Lonely
Alone	Angry	Abused
Resentful	Terrified	Dumped

Adding these words to your feeling vocabulary will help you stay in touch with what you are feeling and help you get through the grieving process.

What Kind of Ex-Wife Are You?

We have categorized a variety of ex-wives based on the circumstances surrounding their marriage and divorce:

- The Princess Bride

- The Where Would You Be Without Me?

- The Working Woman

- The Woman Scorned

- The It's Time to Move On

- The Over the Edge

As you read, determine which one best describes you or your stepwife. If you are a stepmother reading this, don't forget to step into her shoes.

The Princess Bride

> *Denise and Craig were high school sweethearts. When their twenty-two-year marriage fell apart, so did Denise. Her role as mother to her children was the only thing that kept her going. When Craig remarried just eighteen short months after they split up and she had to share her kids with their stepmother, Denise felt she had nothing left.*

Chocolate chip cookies baking in the oven and a cool, refreshing pitcher of lemonade in the fridge: the Princess Bride is the consummate homemaker. The sort of woman who married young and then retired, she has celebrated many anniversaries as a wife and mother, choosing to stay at home and nurture her family rather than work outside the house.

Although the Princess Bride was far more common in the postwar era, there continue to be many households run by these selfless women, who gain much of their self-esteem and pride by immersing themselves in their family's lives. It is easy to see that when a Princess Bride experiences a divorce, she will feel it rip through the very foundation of her being.

A newly divorced Princess Bride has essentially lost her identity. She will probably be more unprepared than any other type of ex-wife to go on with her life and share the role of mother with another woman.

Ex-wives:

- Recapture your self-respect by redefining yourself. Explore work you can do at home, or get some training to prepare yourself for an outside job. Picture yourself out in the world as a competent working woman. Even if money isn't an issue, don't rule out getting a job. Having the sense that you are playing a useful role in society—and that there is something to fall back on in case your situation changes—is always a good idea.

- Nurture your self-esteem by finding some volunteer work to do even if you feel as if you couldn't squeeze one more thing into your day.

- You were probably lucky enough to have your mother or perhaps even a nurse to help out when you became a mother, but your stepwife's mother certainly didn't come to help her when she became a step-mother. Her transition into "motherhood" wasn't nearly as easy as yours, and she may have even become the "new mother" to more than one child, who may not even like her. So as bad as you may be feeling, try to *empathize and acknowledge* what she may be going through.

Stepmothers:

❧ *Empathize and acknowledge feelings* by practicing the following visualization: Imagine you're saddle-training a wild horse. The horse does not want the saddle. He will buck, kick, and rear up on his hind legs when you try to approach him. Ever so slowly, you gain his confidence and trust, until finally he will allow you to be near him. This is the way to gain the trust of a Princess Bride ex-wife: slowly and steadily. If you approach her this way, the odds are greater than she will be able to learn to trust you and may even willingly allow you to share in her most precious treasure, her children.

The Where Would You Be Without Me?

When her husband left her after twenty-five years of marriage, Lana wasn't about to take it lightly. In fact, she would make him pay for the years she sacrificed, giving up her own education and career opportunities. And she didn't care how much it would cost to make sure he understood he couldn't just throw her away like yesterday's garbage.

The Where Would You Be Without Me? ex-wife will be feeling angry, cheated, and taken advantage of. She worked hard to put her husband through school or training for his career. Perhaps she even postponed having children until her husband could contribute financially, easing some of the responsibility she took on. She may have looked forward to staying home to raise children once her husband could support the family or assumed he would support *her* when she was ready to train for her career. Instead she has had a big surprise: divorce has ruined all of her plans.

Ex-wives:

❧ *Empathize and acknowledge feelings.* Even though the best time in your stepwife's life is the worst time in your life, remember she is as entitled to her happiness as you were to yours.

Stepmothers:

❧ Respect your stepwife for how she helped your husband with his career, which you are ultimately benefiting from. If you hear negative things about her, choose to ignore them, and look at the positive signs of the way she lived her life and brought up her children. If she does not feel you judging her, she will be more likely to make room for you.

The Working Woman

Although Margaret hated her job, she hung in there because she had no choice. She was looking forward to be-

coming a stay-at-home mom as soon as her husband got that next promotion. What she got instead was a subpoena informing her that her husband had just filed for divorce.

The 6:00 A.M. alarm rings, and the Working Woman is up and in the shower, readying herself for another eight-hour day at work. Any woman who has juggled a career and a family knows it's not easy, but she's gotten used to it over the years. She may not have homemade chocolate chip cookies waiting for the kids when they get home from school, but she and her husband have learned how to run the household around their busy work schedules. She is an independent woman and can take care of herself and her family. Or can she?

Divorce is a rude awakening for the Working Woman. She finds that working to contribute to the household is a far cry from being the main breadwinner. When it comes time for a spousal or child support settlement, she may feel that she is being penalized for helping the family financially all those years. This will undoubtedly cause anger and bitterness, which can turn to resentment toward her stepwife.

Ex-wives:

◦ Identify some things you can give up, and let go of them. Allow your stepwife to participate in some of the fun things with your kids, which will free you up to have some time for yourself. This will also lessen any resentment the stepmother might be feeling. The kids will benefit because their mom and stepmom are both feeling better—a win-win situation all around.

Stepmothers:

◆§ Make a general offer to help your stepwife get some free time for herself when she feels particularly burned out. Ask if there is anything you can do to help her.

The Woman Scorned

"I don't think I'll ever trust a man again," Edie shared, her voice quivering, at one of our seminars. "I feel betrayed, humiliated, ready to explode, and so depressed. How could I not have known about their affair? How could he do this to me? I hate her! I hate him! I don't think I'll ever get over this."

As the old saying goes, "Hell hath no fury like a woman scorned." Any stepmother who is the other woman, partially responsible for the demise of the ex-wife's marriage, will incur the wrath of the ex-wife. Can a situation like this ever work itself out?

Stepmothers:

◆§ Even though you feel your new husband was unhappy in his marriage and ready to leave her anyway, the truth is—he didn't, that is, not until *you* came along. Something must have been keeping him there, whether it was his fear of leaving and being alone, his guilt, or plain old-fashioned loyalty. And face it: he loved her enough to marry her and have kids with her. It's time to *claim your own baggage.* You were the catalyst in the breakup of the marriage, and now you must be prepared for her rage.

❧ Remember that she is suffering. You are the one in the more secure position. If you step into her shoes, you will understand that because she is feeling so rejected, hurt, and vulnerable, she will be easily threatened, her defenses on high alert, poised to attack at any time.

Ex-wives:

❧ Work hard to *claim your own baggage.* List the ways *you* may have contributed to his leaving, all the things you didn't like about him while you were still married, and the ways your future might be better without him. This will allow you to gain more perspective on the situation and get on with your life.

❧ Remember that no matter how much you hate your ex or stepwife or what you feel they did to you, you still need to *put the kids first.*

It is important to balance out this extremely difficult situation, where one woman is in love and the other woman is in pain over the love she lost.

The It's Time to Move On

It's not always the man who ends the marriage. Many women leave their husbands and have to deal with the broken families they've left behind. But it's never easy to leave your husband and uproot your children. Most ex-wives have no idea what lies in store for them when they choose this route.

When the wife is the one to leave, there can be severe consequences. As the harsh reality of life on her own kicks in, she may find herself clinging to the security of the memories of her old life. Even in the worst relationship, there is some good, and as time passes, ex-wives often find themselves focusing on those good times and glossing over the reasons that they left. She may want her old life back and makes that very clear by trying to stay connected to her ex in any way she can.

Stepmothers, especially all you Wendys, need to understand that over the years, in many ways, two people become one and it's difficult to see your own identity in the relationship. This is particularly true if you married early, as Lynne did, before you have fully defined yourself as a person:

> *Greg was my Dream Prince, and in my eyes he could do no wrong. I loved him with every ounce of my twenty-one-year-old being and knew we would never part. But little by little, his perfection chipped away at my sense of self, until one day I found I no longer had any idea who I was. And although I was still connected to him at my very core, I had to go. Staying with him would have meant the end of me.*

If the It's Time to Move On left her husband for another man, this really complicates the issue, for now she must add guilt to her list of feelings, and men usually behave with rancor in these situations. She should also ask herself why she was unable to leave without a replacement relationship. The stigma is greater for the woman with children who leaves a marriage for another man than it is for the man who leaves for another woman. It is important to remember that she did not create the situation that led up to her exit all by herself.

Ex-wives:

- ❧ *Claim your own baggage.* Although you are the only one who truly understands why you ended your marriage, the truth is, you did it. As a result, you need to *remember realistic expectations* about the way people will respond to you.

Stepmothers:

- ❧ Since you haven't walked in her shoes, be careful how you judge her.

The Over the Edge

Cynthia had repeatedly asked her ex-husband to set aside some time to talk with her about their kids. After being ignored for months, she decided to get back at him and his new wife by dressing her daughter up in her old wedding gown to go trick-or-treating with them. He never even noticed! Had he totally eradicated her from his memory? Furious, Cynthia drove to his house and slashed his tires. This time, she would not *go unnoticed.*

Whether she's a Princess Bride or a Working Woman, she's mad as hell, and she's not going to take it anymore. She may have tried to be accommodating given the situation, but it just didn't get her anywhere. She's been pushed too far, and she snapped. So how did she get this way? She may feel as though she's been squeezed out of her own life and her ex has orchestrated the whole thing. Maybe she has been denied access to her kids or been cheated out of her rightful share of their property. Maybe she's had her nose rubbed in it once too often, and nobody seems to care. She knows it's futile to try to get what she wants through normal channels, so she resorts to taking matters into her own hands.

Every ex-husband seems to have an anecdote about what his ex-wife did to him while they were separating, but there is a point when an ex-wife's pranks become hostile. She may try harassing her ex-husband by doing something like going into the house they once shared and cutting the crotch out of every pair of his pants. It is important to keep an eye on this behavior and watch to see if the pranks escalate to a more serious level.

Stepmothers:

- ❧ It's time to *claim your own baggage.* Are her accusations justified? Have you indeed been trying to stick it to her? If you are in part responsible for her behavior, you need to apologize and stop what you've been doing to provoke her.

- ❧ If your stepwife calls your house in anger, screaming, yelling, and disrupting the tranquility of your household, you may need to *set limits and boundaries* by blocking her phone calls and screening unknown phone numbers on incoming calls.

- ❧ If she's gone completely over the edge and physically assaults you or threatens to, contact your local law enforcement agency or legal representative. You may need to get a restraining order to keep her out of your life. Having the law set *limits and boundaries* will send the message that you are serious and that she needs to leave you alone.

Warning: When pushed too far, the Over the Edge can be potentially dangerous to you and your family. Seek outside help, and remember that just using the PRESCRPTON may not be enough.

Why Can't She Just Get Over It?

Lynne:

> *If I'd only known what to expect after my divorce, I'm pretty sure things wouldn't have hit me so hard. But it seemed that whenever I started feeling a little bit better, something would inevitably come along to knock me back down. No one seemed to understand what I was going through, and to make matters worse, I couldn't stop being angry with myself for not just "getting over it."*

If you are the new (and probably younger) woman in the picture, you are most certainly wondering why his ex-wife doesn't just get over it, especially if she was the one to end the marriage. Perhaps you are thinking that their marriage is ancient history now, and she should just move over and make room for you. After all, *you* didn't have anything to do with their breakup. Why doesn't she just accept it and stop trying to control your life? She obviously couldn't handle her own very well, so why is she messing around with yours? Or if he was the one who ended the marriage, why doesn't she just face it: it's you he loves now, and it's time for her to get a life.

Stepmothers, here's a news flash for you: it just isn't that easy. Every ex-wife reading this book knows how true this statement is. The ex-wife may not even realize exactly why it's so hard to let go after you've come into the picture. Even if the ex-wife was the one who left, she may not be ready to have another woman invading her territory, even if *she* couldn't live there anymore. Remember that having papers that say someone is legally divorced does not guarantee they will be emotionally divorced or even emotionally separated.

Before you can begin mending any break that inevitably occurs between stepwives, you must understand the following reasons as to why she can't just get over it.

It's Genetic

All animals are driven to protect their territory from competitors. Your dog feels afraid when someone enters his territory and expresses his fear by barking, charging, baring his teeth, and, when the perceived danger is extreme, attacking the intruder. Whenever a mammal (no matter what you might call her, your stepwife is still a mammal) experiences a fear response such as this, adrenaline is pumped into the bloodstream, readying the body for a confrontation or an escape. The senses are heightened, and all that matters is survival.

Unlike your own treasured pet, his ex-wife will not bark, charge, or bare her teeth, but she certainly may see you as enough of a threat to her young that she indeed may attack. Ex-wives and stepmothers are natural rivals. Ex-wives, if you feel yourself responding this way, remember the story of King Solomon.

The Old Testament tells us that King Solomon was once faced with making a terrible decision. Two women came to him with a baby, each claiming to be its mother. King Solomon declared that if they could not decide who the mother was, he would cut the child in half, thereby giving each woman part of the child. Upon hearing this, the infant's mother relinquished her claim to the child so he could live. Thus, King Solomon pronounced her to be the real mother.

Ex-wives:

❧ *Putting the kids first* sometimes means letting go. Think about the positive side of things. Be happy that because of your stepwife, your child will be part of a family when he's not with you.

Stepmothers:

❧ This is another occasion for you to *empathize and acknowledge feelings.* By understanding that your mere presence sends up danger signals that often circumvent logic, you will be better equipped to behave in a nonthreatening manner. To disarm your stepwife, make a point of deferring to her in all matters regarding the children, letting her know you honor her position as mother.

Divorce Remorse

Have you ever purchased a big-ticket item, such as a car or a house, and then almost immediately had second thoughts? Were you afraid you'd made a mistake and worried that there was no turning back? If so, you had a case of buyer's remorse, which can be similar to how many ex-wives feel if they've been the one to leave the marriage. But even if it wasn't their choice to leave, divorce remorse may still result, plaguing them with the "I should haves"; "I should have worked harder to keep my marriage together." "I should have seen it coming."

Ex-wives:

✻ You need to *claim your own baggage* by remaining clear about why your marriage didn't work. Write down the ten most negative things about your marriage, how long things were that way, and how you tried to change things.

✻ Whatever you do, *do not* think about the happy, idyllic beginning of your marriage. Instead, remember how it progressed as it went downhill.

Stepmothers:

✻ Clean out your closet. Decide what to keep, what to discard, and what to give away. Pay attention to how emotionally attached you become to something when you think about not having it anymore. Now imagine parting with something as important as a husband and a life. Cut her some slack.

Change

The final reason for the ex-wife's not being able to get over it is the amount of disruption that comes from the changes in her life. The loss can overwhelm even the strongest of women. If you are an ex-wife, take the following quiz by writing yes or no after each question:

Has there been a change in:

1. Your living quarters?
2. Your work life?
3. Your financial security?
4. The amount of help you have with household duties?

5. Child care arrangements?
6. Your economic status?
7. Your emotional support system?
8. Your family system?
9. Your friendships?
10. Your self-image?

Give yourself 10 points for each time you answered yes. Here is the scoring:

10-30 points: You've managed to come out of your divorce relatively unscathed. Consider yourself one of the lucky ones. Call your ex-husband and thank him.

30-70 points: Stability rules. Who said having a career of your own wasn't a good thing? And you probably got to stay in your home. You've still been through enough to make anybody's head spin, so continue *problem-solving* ways to get your life back together.

70-100 points: You have our heartfelt sympathy. You have been through the ringer. Acknowledge yourself for living through such a difficult time in your life. Allow yourself to go through the grief process, and remember to *nurture yourself.*

Commonly Asked Questions

Being an ex-wife is especially confusing when your kids have a stepmother. Ex-wives have many questions about their roles and how to handle their stepwife's intrusion in their life. Following are the most frequently asked questions:

Why does my children's stepmother act as if she's the mother? The stepmom is the mother figure at the father's house. She's probably the one cooking their meals, buying their clothes, or helping with homework, and if she's doing a good job, she begins feeling some ownership toward them. She may even get caught up in the momentum of her mothering tasks and lose sight of what her position really is. Her behavior may be an outgrowth of the genuine care she feels toward your children. And would you really want your ex-husband to be with someone who didn't love your kids?

What gives her the right to criticize my mothering skills? Criticizing or bad-mouthing the mother for not doing things the way *she* does them is something no stepmother has the right to do. If your stepwife seems to have an issue with something you've done, you have the right to remind her gently that *you* are the mother. Although you appreciate what she's doing for your children, you would like her to understand that her role as stepmother does not include an assessment of your mothering skills. Do keep in mind, though, that critical remarks by your stepwife do not necessarily mean she's maliciously trying to push you out of the picture.

Why won't she let me have access to my kids whenever I want it? After divorce, both parents have a right to be with their children. However, having specific dates and times gives children the structure they need in order to live in two different homes and respects the privacy of each parent. Many ex-wives feel they should be entitled to speak with their children whenever they want, but their stepwife is also entitled to be mistress of her own domain. You'll find you'll get much more cooperation from your stepwife if you don't call every time the urge hits you. *Set limits and boundaries* by planning a certain time of the day when you will call, and keep a list of what you wish to say at that time. And if you have e-mail, we strongly encourage you to use it.

·   ·   ·

Once a stepmother enters her stepchildren's lives, complicated feelings of fear, jealousy, and competition will dominate the emotional landscape of most ex-wives and mothers. Even after the ex-wife remarries, she may continue to harbor the passionate feelings that often explode into issues of control and power where her children are concerned. Stepmothers would be wise to keep this in mind and tread lightly. Ex-wives, focus on making your new life, and the lives of your children, as good as they can possibly be. And although your entire life might feel as if it's upside down, treating your stepwife with respect will pay off for you and your kids for years to come.

Chapter 5

Second Wife Syndrome/ Ex–Wife Envy

Close Encounters of the Strange Kind

It's bad enough when you've both married the same guy, but when you and your stepwife live in the same town, frequent the same establishments, and even have the same initials, the prospects for disaster are endless. Sometimes it hits you like a ton of bricks and always at the most inopportune moments, as we discovered. Much to our horror, not only did we share the same husband, it turned out we even had the same gynecologist. We had certifiable cases of Second Wife Syndrome and Ex-Wife Envy.

There are certain classic symptoms that define Second Wife Syndrome and Ex-Wife Envy. For the second wife, it's about playing second fiddle, being compared and confused at every turn, and for the ex-wife it's about replacement.

Louise:

I'd known for years that we had the same gynecologist. I was on hold one day waiting for the nurse to pull my chart so I could set up an appointment, when she came back on the line and said, "How does next Tuesday sound, Lynne?" It was at that exact moment that I realized even my private parts weren't private anymore.

Lynne:

> *Right after Louise and Greg got married, I went to my OB/GYN. I was lying there in my stylish blue hospital gown when the doctor, obviously looking at the wrong chart, entered the room and said, "Louise, how are you today?" How could I let him examine me when he couldn't even tell us apart?*

Second Wife Syndrome

Louise:

> *I had been dangerously close to becoming what every woman nearing thirty dreads: an old maid. And then I met Greg. He was everything I'd ever dreamed of. Well, almost. He did have an ex-wife and a child. But so what? I'd finally met the right guy, and nothing could mar my happiness. So when Greg asked me to move to be closer to him and Evan, I couldn't say yes fast enough.*
>
> *I packed up and prepared to make the most colossal move of my life, one hundred miles away from everything I knew and loved, and I was excited. I couldn't wait for us to be together.*
>
> *As move-in day drew near, however, I began seeing his house, the house I would be moving into, in a whole new light. Although he and Lynne had never lived in this particular house, her essence seemed to be everywhere. Remnants of a life lived together were all over the house: a cutting board with "Lynne & Greg" hand-painted, courtesy of Lynne; dishes they had shared meals on; and even*

> *the bed they had slept in. It suddenly felt as if I couldn't breathe. How could I possibly start fresh in a house filled with vestiges of another woman?*

When you meet that special someone—the man you think you could possibly spend the rest of your life with—all reason and rational thought go out the window. The mundane takes on a distinctively wonderful quality, sleeping becomes impossible, eating unimportant. You're in love. But when that special someone has children, reality, in the shape of his ex-wife, usually has a way of seeping through that reverie of love, and it is not uncommon to experience Second Wife Syndrome before you've even married or met his ex. We hear from women all over the world who are contemplating becoming a second wife, and they ask us, "What am I getting myself into?"

Stepmothers:

⋖ You are entering into an existing family, albeit a broken one, and must *remember realistic expectations* about what this means. You will not only be sharing your everyday life with your stepwife but every major event in your stepchildren's lives as well, including becoming grandparents together someday. Are you ready for that?

⋖ Assess your situation. What exactly is the status of his relationship with his ex? How long were they married? How long have they been apart? How do they communicate? Will you be comfortable with the way things are?

It's understandable to want an exclusive relationship with your husband, but when you try to push his ex-wife out of the picture, you are essentially pushing out the mother of your stepchildren, and this will interfere with the bond between them.

Proceed with Caution

> *Suzette moved into her boyfriend's house—the same house he had shared with his ex-wife, Jaclyn, and their three kids. As bad as that was, what was even worse was that Jaclyn still had her old house key and continued to use it whenever she felt like it.*

You may not be ready to begin a relationship if he hasn't completed his last one. The following is a list of warning signs to be aware of:

- He still resides in the same house as his ex-wife.

- He has been apart from her (and his family) only a very short time.

- He is still plagued by her, constantly talking about her even if only in negative terms.

- He is embroiled in the particulars of ending the marriage.

- They are still conversing at length.

- The ex still has a key to his house.

- There is no set schedule in place regarding the children.

❧ His ex-wife is still considered part of his family; she is included in family events.

❧ His children are nearing puberty. Stepmothers often have more difficulty with older children because they can be more vocal and defiant.

If his situation contains any of these warning signs, you may want to determine if he is even the man for you.

Is He the One for Me? Quiz

The following quiz should give you some insight as to whether he's the man for you. From the list below, circle the ten characteristics and traits most important to you, in a man. Next, rate your man in the ten areas you have chosen, using the following rating system: 1 = poor, 2 = fair, 3 = good, and 4 = excellent.

Characteristic	Rating
Sense of humor	____
Intelligence	____
Flexibility	____
Positive outlook	____
Financial stability	____
Honesty/integrity	____
Energy level	____
Family values	____
Religious beliefs	____
Looks	____
Personality	____
Passion	____
Education	____

Common interests ____
Emotional stability ____
Willingness to participate in
    household chores ____
Creativity ____
Ambition ____
Sensitivity/compassion ____
Understanding ____
Total: ____

Now add up your scores:

40+   The perfect match. You go girl! We hear wedding
       bells. Congratulations.
30-40 A good match. Start looking for that wedding
       dress (but don't have it altered yet).
20-30 A fair match. Proceed with caution. Any extraor-
       dinary circumstances, like an ex-wife and kids
       may set you up to become a statistic. Premarital
       counseling is strongly advised.
0-20   Run quickly, and don't look back. This will *not*
       work under even the best of conditions.

How does your man measure up? If he scored 20 or below,
think very, very carefully about entering into a marriage
with him. Things will be tough enough. Children will only
compound matters drastically.

The Used Car
You don't like his ex-wife, and she doesn't like you. Even if
you started off on a friendly note, even if several years have
passed, it doesn't seem to make any difference. Her presence is a constant reminder that the perfect life you envi-
sioned is flawed. Face it: you've bought yourself a used car,

and although it may look brand-new, it's got some miles on it. It could use a little touch-up paint, and when you get it home, you even discover an old pair of sunglasses in the glove compartment. In other words, your husband comes with a lot of baggage; he is encumbered. Even understanding this, you may still feel certain undeniable emotions when it comes to your stepwife.

Whether or not you want to admit it, you feel competitive and threatened, even though their marriage is over. They can't stand each other, and yet *still* you feel threatened. Could it be because she was there first and they have a history and children together? Does he love you as much as he loved her? Will you have children together too? What if they rekindle their love for each other? What if they decide to work things out? Will his friends and family love and accept you as much as they did her?

No matter how hard you try to put these feelings aside, they are natural when two women are fighting for the attention of the same man.

Stepmothers:

⋯s Acknowledge that you feel threatened and competitive. *Remember realistic expectations* regarding the relationship your husband had with his ex-wife. You need to relax and trust that your relationship is strong and real. Their marriage didn't work. You represent a new beginning in your husband's life, so nurture your new relationship, and above all, don't let your stepwife come between you.

⋯s You will damage what you have if you allow yourself to be jealous of what they had. Understand that as you

live your life together, your history with him will develop. You and your stepwife are two different people
and will experience life differently, even though it is
with the same guy. Respect that she is his past, and remember that you are his present and future.

- ⚘ Your stepwife is entitled to have a relationship with
  her ex. They have children together, and as responsible parents they need to *talk and communicate effectively about those children.* If you feel she is taking
  advantage of the situation, wanting more than a relationship as parents, then it's time to *set limits and
  boundaries.*

All's Unfair In Love and War

If you notice yourself feeling angry and hostile much of
the time, you may be wondering why she's still in his life and
why she's allowed to make your life so miserable. Before you
can answer these questions, you must first understand why
she does the things she does. Review Chapter 4. Keep in
mind, though, that you have what she might still want. She
might not have yet acknowledged that her marriage is over,
and she could be in a very bad place. Would you want to be in
her shoes? And if you were, how would you behave?

Stepmothers:

- ⚘ *Remember realistic expectations.* As a second wife,
  you may have to give up some of the expectations that
  come with being a first wife, like being his one and
  only. Realize that your courtship will include his children and ex-wife. Concentrate on what you are gaining, not losing. Consider the possibility that she broke

him in for you, and now you get to reap the rewards of her years of hard work and, yes, even nagging. Hopefully, your man has learned from his past mistakes and will enter into your relationship cognizant of what he can do differently the second time around.

A stepmother can sometimes feel little to no sympathy for her stepwife, and it makes sense that it would be so. She's heard all the stories about the ex-wife, but not from her stepwife's perspective. Furthermore, as a stepmother, being naturally competitive, you want to believe the worst, so you do. Now is your chance to rise above this, step into her shoes, and work toward a positive relationship with her. You may even want to acknowledge to her that although you are not prepared to hear her side, you do understand that there are two sides to every story.

Ex-Wife Envy

Traditionally, for there to have been a stepmother, the biological mother would have to have died. We firmly believe that if ghosts do exist, former wives haunted their widowed husbands who remarried, envious throughout all eternity of the women who replaced them in the hearts of their husband and children.

Lynne:

> *I'll never forget the first time I saw Greg and Evan and Louise together. It was a picture-perfect Sunday afternoon, the kind that makes your heart rejoice at simply being alive. And to make it all even better, I was going out on a date.*

As the oldies tunes played, we cruised around town in his sporty red convertible, and when my date pulled up to the stop sign just ahead, I remember breathing a sigh of relief because the bad times finally seemed to be behind me. But as I turned my head to look into the intersection, I saw Evan walking between Greg and Louise, holding hands, swinging their arms back and forth, happy as could be, as they walked across the street.

The lump in my throat was so big it was a few minutes before I could ask my date to take me home. It was all over for me. It was days before I could shake the image of my little boy holding the hand of the woman who had caused me such pain.

Starting Over

Donna was twenty-four years old when her parents split up. Occasionally, Donna's mother would ask about her ex and his new wife. When she found out Donna's father had lost weight and was traveling the world, she was fit to be tied. "That s.o.b. I begged him to get in shape and spend more time with me. Why couldn't he have done all that when we were together?"

The marriage of your ex-husband signals a new beginning for him and the absolute end of your marriage for you. Your husband has moved on, and he probably moved on first. Maybe he's recreated himself, doing things he never considered while married to you.

There are many eligible women out there, and your ex will never be lonely. And wouldn't you know it, just about the time you start to accept the idea of being an ex-wife, boom! you're a stepwife too. Whether you've been apart six months or six years, you and your ex-husband have an established way of dealing with each other, and although you may not always like it, you've become comfortable with your way of doing things. But now the rules have changed. Whatever arrangements you and he had no longer apply because *she* is in the picture.

Ex-wives:

❧ When your ex-husband remarries, his considerations for you will change. There's a new woman in his life, and you need to make room for her. His loyalty lies with her now, and in the interest of *putting your kids first,* you must understand that you will be taking a back seat. This is a very good time to *set limits and boundaries* regarding everyone's roles.

❧ Remember that your stepwife has all kinds of adjustments of her own to make. She's a new wife, a stepmother, and a stepwife, all at the same time. Unlike when you married and were able to have all your husband's love and attention, she must share him with you and your kids. Try to empathize with what she's going through, and cut her some slack.

She's Young and Sexy

If you're older than your stepwife, try not to get into a competition over looks or who has more sex appeal. It's unproductive and a good way to lose self-esteem. We know you're angry. His life just keeps getting better, while yours only gets harder. Why is it that men improve as they get older and women just . . . get older. And why can they be with a woman who ranges anywhere from twenty years younger to twenty years older when we have a hard time finding a man? It does seem that the clock ticks faster for women, but this is your opportunity to overcome those old stereotypes.

Ex-wives:

- *Nurture yourself.* There may be nobody around to do it for you, so you really have to take care of yourself. Start exercising. Schedule a spa treatment. You're probably missing the physicality of your marriage, so get a massage. A massage therapist can work your back better than your ex-husband ever could.

- *Put your kids first.* Always make the best of it in front of your children. By watching you, they will learn important coping skills that will stay with them for life.

- *Claim your own baggage.* Don't punish your stepwife for your insecurities if she happens to be young and beautiful. It's almost expected a man will marry a younger woman the second time. Consider the possibility of how much worse you would feel if he had replaced you with someone older and more accomplished than you.

Stepmothers:

- Do not flaunt or taunt your stepwife with your youth. This is unkind and will only make you look petty and immature and incite your stepwife as well.

I Only Want Him Because Somebody Else Has Him

One of the stepwives we've consulted with:

I'm married to a man with three kids whose wife left him for another man. As soon as he and I got together, she wanted him back, and he wasn't interested. Now she's doing everything she can to make our lives miserable.

Think about having a garage sale to get rid of all the old junk you no longer want or need. You clean the stuff up, place an ad in the paper, put up a sign or two, and you're in business. As soon as the first customer arrives and makes an offer on your old decoupage ashtray, doesn't it suddenly take on a new glow? How is it you never noticed the leaning tower of Pisa on the front? Remembering the summer you spent in Italy, you now wonder how you could ever part with such a treasure. You tell your customer there's been a mistake. The ashtray is no longer for sale. This is human nature in its simplest form: the perceived value of an object increases along with the number of its admirers.

Ex-wives:

❦ Be honest and *claim your own baggage.* If you kept that old ashtray wouldn't it still be in the garage today collecting dust? Do you really want your ex-husband back? Even though another woman has cleaned him up, he's still that same old guy he was last week, last month, last year. Even if she has him now and you still don't have anyone new, you're relationship didn't work then, and it probably wouldn't work any better now. It's time to let go and move on.

They're My Flesh and Blood

The hardest part of divorce, ex-wives tell us, is having to give up their children, whether every other weekend or every other week. It is, after all, the mother who carries the child in her body, right below her heart, for nine months. It's bad enough to have to share your children with their father, but it is unthinkable to have another woman tucking them in at night, comforting them when they're sick or upset, or even replacing you in their hearts. The agony of having a woman you don't even know, let alone like, performing functions that you feel should be yours alone, can make a mother come unglued.

Ex-wives:

- It is okay to feel out of control. It is *not* okay to behave that way. We know that often mothers behave badly because they are terrified of losing their children to their stepwife. Trying to control those around you will not make the situation any better. It will only cause everyone, especially your children, anxiety and unhappiness. Respect yourself enough to know that your children could never love another woman the way they love you. The bond between a mother and her children is something that nothing and no one can break.

- Believe it or not, most stepmothers do not want to be their stepchildren's mother. They just want to be the best stepmother they can be. By *claiming your own baggage* concerning your fears, you will hopefully someday be able to view your stepwife as an ally rather than an enemy out to take what is yours. The more people who love your kids, the better off your kids will be.

Nothing Is Sacred

Maybe it's not just the physical presence of your stepwife that you resent. It could be the fact that she's driving your old car, using your old stuff, and maybe even living in your old house. You visualize her entertaining on the couch you picked out, serving drinks in your old wine glasses, and even sleeping in your old bed. You're furious. You have truly been replaced in every aspect of your life. Nothing is sacred.

Ex-wives:

- Believe us when we tell you that your stepwife does not want your old stuff, and she wants to live in your old house even less. In fact, she would be happy if you would come and take back anything and everything that was yours (not your ex-husband, of course). Don't resent her for having your things. Empathize with how hard it must be for her to live in another woman's house, with another woman's belongings.

- The possessions you acquire in a marriage belong to both parties. If your stepwife is unlucky enough to have to live with your old stuff, remember that it was your ex-husband's old stuff too and he is entitled to sit on that couch and drink out of those wine glasses if that's the way you divided everything up.

You Mean She Gets the Friends Too?

There are so many casualties of divorce, friends being just one. We know how incredibly painful it can be when you find out that your friends are now her friends. Didn't all those years of friendship mean anything? Why does it feel that your friends chose your ex and stepwife over you?

Ex-wives:

- Your friends are also your ex-husband's friends, and they shouldn't be put in the position of taking sides between stepwives. This is a very sensitive situation and must be handled delicately. *Set limits and boundaries* by not quizzing your friends as to what your ex and stepwife are up to or how often they all get together. This is sure to make them uncomfortable and could possibly come between you and them.

- You need to help your friends problem-solve so they can remain connected with "both sides." Let them know that it's okay to invite your ex-husband and stepwife to gatherings. Obviously, you'd rather they didn't, but *remembering realistic expectations* may save you from being the one without an invitation.

- As painful as it is, you need to *empathize and acknowledge* your stepwife's position. Why shouldn't she forge friendships with her husband's friends especially if those people encourage and welcome it?

- Expand your horizons. Meet new people, and make new friends. Join an organization where you have something in common with the people there—perhaps the Sierra Club if you like the outdoors or Parents Without Partners so you can meet other single parents. This will help fill any gap in your social life.

Losing Ground

It seems as if no one gives ex-wives credit anymore for having territorial feelings about their children. The current thinking is that fathers are just as important to their development. Whatever happened to the mother-child bond we used to hear so much about?

Mothers have lost some ground as custodial parents. Today's system has elevated the importance of fathers, and when a divorced man assumes the responsibilities that mothers traditionally carried out, kudos are liberally heaped on him. Being a single father can even make him attractive to some women. Yet when a woman becomes a single mother, who acknowledges her? Certainly not the men who refuse to date women with children. Divorced mothers need to be acknowledged for the heavy load they carry; instead, they often feel ganged up on and abused.

Ex-wives usually take great satisfaction in the difficulties stepmothers encounter. They didn't ask for this woman to be in their lives. As far as they're concerned, she deserves everything that happens to her. They hope she may not be around that long. But think about it. If your husband and your stepwife get a divorce, your children will have to go through the trauma of yet another divorce. Your ex will eventually find another woman, and you'll have to go through this again. Is that what you really want? You now have the opportunity to begin a whole new chapter in your life. And when you look into the faces of your children, keep in mind that you wouldn't have them if it weren't for him.

You're in It Together

Like it or not, you're in this together. Second Wife Syndrome and Ex-Wife Envy are difficult to dismiss because of the constant reinforcement—whether it's being mistaken for each other at the gynecologist or having one of his friends call you by *her* name. It's amazing how many people unwittingly say the wrong thing, which can send a stepwife into a frenzy.

Commonly Asked Questions

Whose life is it anyway? Reality check: You are not the only woman in your family, and you never will be as long as you have a stepwife. The moment he said *I do* for the second time, you became part of an extended-blended family, fated to share the small world in which you all live. You need to find a way to make the best of it.

Do I have the temperament to deal with Second Wife Syndrome, and why does Ex-Wife Envy hit some people harder than others? Women who suffer greatly from Second Wife Syndrome and Ex-Wife Envy will have similar attributes:

Birth Order

First born, subject to replacement issues
Only child, not used to sharing
The baby of the family, always got your own way

Personality Traits

Naturally competitive
Self-involved
Temperamental
Prone to overreacting
High-strung
Frequently feel insecure

Like being in control
Like to feel special
Tendency toward feeling like a victim
Thrive on structure and consistency

Those of you who are already stepwives will need to work hard to overcome the strikes you have against you and develop the skills you need to counteract your natural personality. If you are soon to be a stepmother, you may want to reconsider your impending marriage.

Fighting against the unfairness of your situation will never make it go away. But if you really want to stop feeling like a victim of your own circumstances, use the knowledge we've given you in this chapter.

Chapter 6

The First Step

How can you think about becoming CoMamas when your stepwife hates you or you've never even spoken to each other? We promise that even if you are the only one to make an effort, you can change your stepwife relationship. The secret to becoming CoMamas lies in learning these communication techniques and applying them in an emphathetic style. Our advice will work whether your stepwife lives in the same city or another state, and our techniques can even be practiced in a phone conversation. Getting started isn't easy, as our years of miscommunication showed.

If You Can't Say Something Nice

Lynne:

> Before the divorce, Karen and I were acquaintances and our sons friends. On this particular day, I arrived at her house to pick up Evan. According to the plan we'd made, there would be a babysitter, and Karen wouldn't be home when I got there to pick him up. When I knocked on the door, much to my surprise not only was Karen standing in front of me, Louise was right next to her! I was caught completely off-guard. Where was the babysitter? Looking straight at Louise, I sputtered "What are you doing here?" I've forgotten by now exactly what her response was, but I can tell you it was anything but nice.

Louise:

> *After Greg and I married, Karen and I became friends. We had gone shopping that day but arrived back at her house earlier than expected. We were standing in her hallway when suddenly the door opened, and I heard, "Is anybody home?" I turned to look, not believing my eyes when I saw Lynne standing there! "What are you doing here?" she asked in a very accusatory tone of voice—as if I had no right to be at Karen's house. I couldn't even respond I was so shocked to see her.*

Lynne's reaction to seeing Louise in Karen's house was one of surprise. Louise thought she was being accused of doing something wrong. Be mindful of listening carefully because it is very easy to misinterpret even the slightest gesture or tone of voice from your stepwife.

Yabba–Dabba–Doo . . .

When a caveman drew his eyebrows together and scowled, this was a clear message to would-be trespassers: Stay away. And when a baby turns down his lower lip, his mother knows something is wrong. Is he hungry? Sick? Does his diaper need changing?

Facial expressions, tone of voice, and gestures—body language—are what communication is all about. Although we use words to express ourselves, the added component of body language enhances what we say. According to Dr. Albert Mehrabian of the University of California at Los Angeles, only 7 percent of the meaning of a message is carried in the words we speak. Thirty-eight percent is carried in the tone of voice we use, which helps us make sense of the message. Body language accounts for the remaining 55 percent.

So remember that it's not always what you're saying but how you're saying it that will have the biggest impact on your stepwife.

The Basic Five

> *Laura arrived at school for the science fair and spotted Ned's ex-wife, Beth, immediately. Although she didn't speak a single word to Laura, Beth made it clear that Laura's presence was not wanted. She never made eye contact, and whenever Laura spoke she "politely" ignored her, making Laura feel like a complete outsider.*

It's the little things that really make us crazy. And whether you want to admit it or not, it's the little things that make or break a relationship. "She looked at me funny" or "I saw her roll her eyes at me when I spoke" have been enough to induce stepwives to wage all-out war. Stepwives are very likely to display the look of fear, hate, or displeasure; it is a primitive language of feelings and emotions that speaks volumes even when you're silent. Because your stepwife sees you as a potential threat and is vigilant when you're around, she'll be watching and listening intently to the language of your feelings, ready to pounce on your every gesture or tone.

Even when you can successfully control what comes out of your mouth, controlling your body language and tone of voice is another thing altogether. You just can't help yourself: when you see her, you tense up, your palms sweat, and your facial expression hardens to a scowl. You feel that the only way to hide your feelings is to ignore her—pretend she doesn't exist, and maybe she'll go away.

Unfortunately, ignoring her won't solve the problem because stepwives constantly tell us they feel slighted and insulted when they aren't acknowledged. If this is the way you've been handling your stepwife, you can make an immediate improvement in your situation by changing a few simple behaviors that we call the Basic Five:

1. Smile.
2. Make eye contact.
3. Say, "Hello, [her name]."
4. Be aware of your body language.
5. If others are present, introduce and include your stepwife in the conversation.

Although the Basic Five seem ridiculously obvious, it's astounding how often these simple courtesies are lacking in a stepwife encounter. These common social graces that we extend to our acquaintances are never extended to our stepwives. Why? Because we don't usually smile and speak to people we don't like. But unless you remain actively aware and work on suppressing those natural urges, you will automatically give her ammunition to use against you. She will accuse you of being rude, and she will be right. We speak from experience. By not using the Basic Five, we added years to our conflicts.

As you become more and more a part of each other's lives at birthdays, graduations, and weddings, difficult situations will continue to arise. When these situations take place, using the Basic Five—the little courtesies you would extend to any other member of the human race—will go a long way toward disarming your stepwife.

Stepwives:

☙ If you have trouble countering your natural impulses when you see your stepwife, pretend she's an acquaintance you've met on the street. "Hello, how are you?" "Nice day today, isn't it?" are appropriate salutations.

Ex-wives:

❧ Imagine a friend has agreed to watch your children while you go out of town. How would you behave? Would you thank her? Thinking of your stepwife as someone who is helping you with your kids when you can't be there will help you feel more like acknowledging her contributions.

Setting the Stage

Sometimes the Basic Five just aren't enough, and you need to go further. You may need to have a conversation longer than one or two sentences with her. But how do you open up the lines of communication when your words stick in your throat? Remember that these are physiological responses that accompany primal feelings, but you can overcome them if you are willing to work on it.

Stepwives:

❧ Send her a note asking to get together in a neutral spot. Your note should read something like this: "I know it isn't easy for either of us to be in each other's lives, so I'd like to try and do all I can to make it better for all of us. Would you be willing to meet me so we can work on it?"

❧ Designate a start and stop time for your meeting—perhaps just prior to picking up the kids. Just like the blind date you're not sure about, a time limit guarantees an easy exit if things don't go as well as you'd planned.

❧ Think about what you want to say at the meeting, and write it down for yourself, using "I" statements, ensuring you will *talk and communicate effectively.* *Do* say "I feel that I'd like to have a better relationship with you." *Don't* say: "You make me feel horrible when you don't talk to me." Would you be receptive if she were saying the same thing to you in the same way?

What is the best you can hope for from your first meeting? Focus on setting a civilized, friendly tone that will allow you to work together, and remember that becoming CoMamas is a process that takes place over time. Be patient. Keep your goal in mind, and you won't hinder the process.

Getting Down to the Real Nuts and Bolts

So here you are, face to face, with no one else around for support for maybe the first time. The way you handle yourself at this meeting will have a direct effect on the relationship you are about to create. Remember that you will want to have other meetings to work out your issues, and you need her to be willing to come back to the table at a later date, so go easy on her. Consider bringing your stepwife a copy of this book, so she can be just as informed as you are.

This meeting will go more smoothly if you remember that some topics are taboo.

Ex-wives:

Don't tell her about your past relationship with your ex-husband. Believe us, she doesn't want to hear about the good, the bad, or the ugly. Taking her on a trip down memory lane will only put her on the defensive, so keep this information to yourself.

Don't talk to her about what you see as your ex-husband's negative qualities. She will feel the need to protect him and may let you know that in no uncertain terms.

Don't share anything about any feelings of love you may still feel toward your ex, unless you are trying to make her feel even more threatened than she already does. Keep in mind that you are trying to calm her fears, not rekindle them.

Don't offer suggestions about how she can be a good wife to your ex, even though you may have been married to him for a long time and may feel you know him better than she does.

Don't even bring up the issue of spousal and child support. This is between you and your ex-husband, and bringing it up will only cause a further breakdown in communication. Don't forget that his money is now her money.

Stepmothers:

Don't talk about how happily married you are or how wonderful you think your new husband is. The last thing she wants to hear about is your "happily ever after" when hers didn't work.

Don't tell her about special moments with your stepchildren unless you want to get nowhere fast. At this early point in your relationship, she will find it too painful and may retaliate.

Don't tell her details about the social life you and your husband now share. Hearing for the first time or the second, as her friends might have already told her, that her friends are now your friends is bound to cause her pain and will only set you back in your attempts to form a working relationship.

Don't analyze what you think went wrong with her marriage and why it didn't work. Even if it makes you feel better, it's really between your stepwife and her ex.

Keep this first meeting light, and keep it positive. Use the following questions and statements to keep yourself on the right track: "How do you see me fitting into your and your child's life?" "What do you expect of me?" "Are you willing to help me make things better?"

Taking It One Step Further

Your first meeting was a success, and your stepwife has agreed to another one. Now where do you go from here? Do you continue to stay on an upbeat note, or turn it up a notch by discussing the things that bother you? The answer to these questions depends on how your relationship is progressing.

If there's nothing in particular that is really bothering you (that would be rare indeed), just go ahead and keep it superficial. But if her behavior is really driving you crazy, this second meeting is the time to deal with it. Be brave and forge ahead, but not without some helpful hints:

❧ When you invite her to this next meeting, let her know how happy you were with the outcome of the last one. Share with her (but only if you want to) that you are using the CoMamas PRESCRPTON. Tell her you are ready to *claim your own baggage* by accepting your part in the continuing problem. Ask her to come to the meeting ready to talk to you about *one* thing you do that she positively can't stand. This is your chance to set a good example.

❧ Prepare for the meeting ahead of time, as you should every time you're in contact. Decide exactly what it is she does that pushes your buttons the hardest. Does she fail to acknowledge you in public or in private? Does she cross your boundaries by scheduling appointments for the kids during your time with them without checking with you first? Be very specific.

❧ Continue *problem-solving* by prioritizing these in order of how much they bother you. Pick the one that is the most annoying to you and practice using "I" statements that will best express how her behavior makes you feel and what you would like her to do to improve the situation—for example, "I am more than happy to take Noah to the doctor, but I feel discounted when you schedule appointments for him during my time because my schedule is so tight. I would really appreciate it if you would check with me before you set up any appointments when he's with me."

❧ Think about what it is that bothers her about you. We think you probably know. This way you will be more prepared to hear what she has to say.

❧ Practice what you want to say in front of a mirror and with a tape recorder to make sure you're not letting your tone of voice or body language do your talking for you.

The Second Meeting

The day of reckoning has arrived. Give yourself points for doing everything within your power to transform this second meeting into a win for both of you:

🙚 Don't leave matters to chance. Remember the Basic Five, and greet your stepwife cordially. Thank her for getting together with you a second time. Tell her how much you respect her willingness to work out your problems.

🙚 Encourage her to begin telling you what bothers her the most about you. Let her know how important it is for you to hear what *you* can do to rectify the state of affairs between the two of you. Breathe deeply, and if you feel your temper being triggered, practice self-control techniques (see Chapter 7). You *can* do this!

🙚 If your stepwife hasn't read this book, she may not give it to you in "I" statements, so it's up to you to *talk and communicate effectively* by using reflective listening and clarification—for example, "You seem to be upset, and I'm not quite sure I understand what you're asking me to do. Are you saying that you want me to say 'Hello' when I see you?" or "I'm sorry you're upset, and I'd like to work it out. Please let me know specifically what you're asking of me."

🙚 Her words might sting, and you may have to try very hard not to take her message personally, but once she knows you understand how she feels, you're almost home free.

❧ After you hear her out, it's okay for you to ask for a little time out to really think about what she said—for example, "I hear what you're saying. Would you mind if I
take a few minutes to think about it?"

❧ Now is the time to *empathize and acknowledge feelings.* You may want to say, "I've had the feeling of not
being acknowledged, and I know how bad that can
feel. I'm sorry I made you feel that way. How would you
like me to acknowledge you?"

❧ If you feel the words of acknowledgment sticking in
your throat, think about how good it feels when you're
acknowledged. Now go ahead and do it. Say something nice to your stepwife even if you can't make your
voice match your words. In time, if you keep practicing acknowledgment, you may find your words ring-
ing with sincerity.

This is where things can get sticky. Perhaps you'd like to
bring up some things she did in the past that made you feel
she didn't deserve to be acknowledged. Whatever you do,
don't do this. It will only keep the fighting alive. Stick to the
present and the intentions that are on the table today.

Be prepared for backsliding to occur at any time, even
during this meeting. Whenever people are learning new behaviors, they sometimes revert to the old ones without even
realizing it. Remember to give each other the benefit of the
doubt rather than condemn the other person for their mistakes.

Now it's your turn to tell her the one thing you would like
her to change and get her agreement to change it. You
claimed your own baggage, and it's time for her to claim hers.

124 *$ Stepwives*

You both should be feeling a little bit of relief at this point at being able to discuss what's bothering you about the other person. Now you can stop blaming each other. You've both been right, and you've both been wrong numerous times in the past. Give each other that, and get on with the business of cooperating.

Settle on how long you'll work on your issues before meeting again. Set up a time to follow up and review your progress. This could be anywhere from two weeks to two months, depending on the amount of interaction you normally have with each other. The general rule is that the more you interact with each other, the more problems will surface, so meetings should be scheduled closer together.

Hold each other accountable only for the one thing you've agreed to work on. For example, if your one request from your stepwife is that she not schedule appointments on your time and she doesn't, she has lived up to her commitment. Even if she bad-mouths you or does something else that makes you angry during this period of time, she has honored her agreement for this one issue, and you should be one step closer to establishing trust. Continue with this process until you have a relationship that allows you to co-parent in a healthy, respectful manner—until you have become CoMamas.

If you lose your cool, try to recognize it early on. Apologize for your words or behavior, and let your stepwife know you still want to work on the relationship. If you are not able to calm yourself during your meeting, let your stepwife know that you need to take a break. Take some time for yourself, and then call her back and apologize. Let her know how important it is to work together for the children's sake and that this is a challenging process that will take some time. *Claim your own baggage.* Make another date with a smaller, more workable agenda that has a better chance of ending in success.

What most stepwives have discovered is that when they start making progress on the behavior that sets them off the most, there aren't as many issues as they originally thought. You may even find you really can live quite comfortably with many of her minor annoyances. And if you accept hers, she might even accept yours.

I've Tried All That, and It Just Didn't Work

Let's be honest: this all sounds great, but what happens when your stepwife refuses to meet with you? What can you possibly do then? Can you work the PRESCRPTON all by yourself?

The answer here is a definite *yes!* We work with many mothers and stepmothers whose stepwives have no idea the other is working the CoMamas program, and in most cases there has been improvement. Often, stepwives begin to feel better as soon as they develop some empathy and begin to understand just why *she* behaves the way she does. And when one person improves her behavior, the other will eventually respond positively. Because your stepwife may still be pretty tough on you, it will take some time for her to notice that you are behaving differently, and in the meantime, she may sling a few arrows your way. *Remembering realistic expectations* will prepare you to stay the course even if she pushes you off.

Before You Get to the Altar

Stepmothers-to-be often ask us if it's appropriate for them to begin working the PRESCRPTON before they reach the altar. In answer, we invite them to our seminars. This is the very best time to anticipate and prevent stepwife wounds—*before* they occur. When we have worked with women before they marry, they have the advantage of knowing what problems will inevitably crop up and can keep them to a minimum.

Commonly Asked Questions

When you decide to use the Basic Five and begin *talking and communicating effectively* with your stepwife, you take your first steps down that long road to becoming CoMamas. If you don't allow your stepwife to know how you honestly feel, how can she ever change the behavior that's bothering you? We're often asked the following questions about communication between stepwives:

Do we need to be friends? Since we have become CoMamas, people frequently ask us if we are friends. But being friends isn't what CoMamas is all about. CoMamas means instead that you are friendly enough to work together to *put the kids first* in every way you can—no more and no less.

When should the kids be told we're communicating? If you are both actively working the PRESCRPTON and have managed to continue to *talk and communicate effectively,* we recommend you wait until you've worked through the expected episodes of backsliding before telling the kids what you're doing. You don't want them to get their hopes up, only to have them dashed. And when you see the changes that come over them once they are no longer trapped between two women at war, you will be even more motivated to keep up your good work. Seeing the burden of their entrapment being lifted from their shoulders is one of the rewards of being CoMamas.

Is it a good idea to set up regular meetings even after we've become CoMamas? Not everyone can do it, but we highly recommend having continued meetings where you can *talk and communicate effectively.* Having this in place will provide a release and a forum to remind each other of the agreements you made. Being open with your feelings is a must in the stepwife relationship, as long as you are respectful. But we know all too well that this is anything but easy. By not speaking up, you cheat her of her chance to be a problem solver and not just a problem. And since your stepwife is not a mind reader, it's up to you to take responsibility for letting her know how she can help change the negative energy between you.

If you find you are working the PRESCRPTON by yourself before you become a stepwife, consider yourself very lucky. Our hope is that you won't ever be forced to suffer through years of agony and conflict as so many of us have.

Chapter 7

The Man in the Middle and the Man on the Outside

> *Doug was dreading his son Eli's seventh birthday party. It meant another showdown between Eli's mother, Corrine, and his stepmother, Eva, which he, as Man in the Middle, would have to referee.*
>
> *Doug and Eva had been married two years and she had yet to attend one of Eli's birthday parties because Corrine didn't want her there. But this year, Eva put Doug on notice: she demanded to be included—or else.*
>
> *Doug was fed up being in the middle of the constant bickering between Corrine and Eva, and so he came up with a plan: he and Eva would host the birthday party on odd-numbered years, and Corrine could host on the even-numbered. It might not have been the perfect solution, but he needed to do something to escape from the pressure cooker his life had become because of these two women.*

The Man in the Middle is the man responsible for bringing the stepwives together in the first place. His counterpart is the Man on the Outside—the man who either marries or has a relationship with the ex-wife. Although we've spoken to many men in the stepwife arena, it is the extensive work that Dr. Krausz has conducted in counseling couples that has helped us to illuminate the behavior of the men profiled throughout this chapter. It is important for step-wives to understand what makes these men tick and how to cope with them. Stepwives, we encourage—maybe even dare—you to ask your men to read this chapter.

The Man in the Middle

Diplomatic. Fair-minded. Superhuman. These are just a few of the qualities the Man in the Middle needs to possess if stepwives are to survive the explosion created by divorce and remarriage. Pushed and pulled, insulted and assaulted, he often appears tired, frayed, and rough around the edges. He has a wife, an ex-wife, and children, all vying for his attention. And often most of them don't get along with each other. So short of enrolling in training as a referee, what is the poor guy to do?

The Man in the Middle can make or break the stepwife relationship by fanning the fires of jealousy and competition—or creating a healthy, balanced atmosphere where stepwives can work out their differences. Sometimes it's hard for women to remember that men also have feelings and that it's often difficult for them to express themselves. Stepwives need to listen and carefully observe to gauge what is truly on his mind. If you pay close attention, you may find that not only is his road just as difficult as yours, but that his feelings aren't all that different.

Men in the Middle have revealed to us that they often feel:

Torn	Afraid	Angry
Manipulated	Resentful	Defeated
Guilty	Powerless	Criticized
Overwhelmed	Assaulted	Wronged
Inadequate	Burdened	Obligated

Previous life experiences will determine the type of Man in the Middle your man becomes. We are all shaped by the negative and positive messages we received as children, which may cause problems in any relationship. As adults, when situations are less complicated, we are better equipped to control the negative influences of our past. The stepwife relationship, anything but uncomplicated, may cause the Man in the Middle to revert to old childhood patterns. Check off any of the family behaviors that may affect your Man in the Middle:

___There was so much commotion in his life he couldn't think.

___Problems were always swept under the rug.

___The relationships in his family were distant and detached.

___He was disciplined through intimidation.

___He tries to say what a person wants to hear to avoid conflict.

___He's afraid to make his own decisions.

___He never had any fun with his family.

___He never saw his parents display affection.

___He's afraid to do the unfamiliar.

___His parents beat him, but he felt he deserved it.

___His dad used to hit his mom.

___His parents' love for him ran hot and cold.

As the ex-wife, you need to remember that while you were married to him, you probably felt empathy for the hurts your ex-husband experienced as a child. But at this point, you may be so far removed from any empathetic feelings toward him that you use this information as a weapon against him.

Focus on the behavior you checked off, and see if you can re-capture the empathy you once felt. It doesn't matter if you feel he has earned every one of your bad feelings toward him. If you want your life to get easier, you will have to stop seeing him as an adversary.

Why He Hates His Ex-Wife

Ex-wives are not the only ones who lose in a divorce. The ramifications are often just as far reaching for men. Love and money—issues that cause arguments during marriage—are magnified after divorce. The Man in the Middle's feel-ings toward his ex-wife will be formed not only by his previous influences, but also by what happened during the breakup and how it was settled in court. And if his ex-wife has done any one of the following, he may hate her with a vengeance:

❧ Left him for another guy. Nothing is as damaging to a man's ego as being thrown over for another man. He'll hate her now, and maybe even forever. These feelings can override his natural instincts as protector and provider, and he will look at spousal and sometimes even child support as a personal affront.

❧ Bleeding him dry. The legal system has had a ten-dency to rule in favor of the woman, and although rul-ings increasingly have been in the husband's favor, this continues to be a sore spot for divorced men everywhere. Most men don't have a problem paying what they feel is their fair share. But when a woman works the system by holding the man completely ac-countable for her lifestyle, he feels as if he can't get a break anywhere, and his emotional temperature will rise.

❧ Taunting him. He left her and tried to do the right thing by making it up to her in overly generous support payments. But when she taunts him with the fact that he wouldn't be paying at all if he'd stuck around, his anger begins to overshadow any feelings of guilt he may be experiencing.

❧ Won't let him see his children. Now she's gone too far, and he will either do everything in his power to fight back or slink away in defeat. Somehow he can't make her play fair even though he may be sticking to his end of the bargain by handing over regular child support payments.

What Kind of Man in the Middle Is He?

We hear from a lot of men, and we are always pleased to see so many attending our workshops and support groups. The CoMamas philosophy has always been that children need both their mothers and fathers, and if you are the Man in the Middle reading this, we commend you for sticking around and being in your kids' lives. You will never be sorry that you chose this course.

Stepwives around the world have described the many types of Men in the Middle who have affected their lives. We find that the majority of divorced men fall into one or more of the following categories:

❧ The Tightrope Walker

❧ The Chameleon

- ❧ The I Need a Wife

- ❧ The Do What I Say or Else

The Tightrope Walker

Nicki came to us ready to throw in the towel on her marriage of just one year. She was devastated because her husband, Peter, had turned on her, yelling at her more than he had ever yelled at his ex-wife, Stacy. Why was he treating her like the enemy when she was just telling him how he should handle Stacy, the real enemy?

Performing a balancing act like no other, the Tightrope Walker is one of those brave souls who dares to walk that oh-so-fine line between stepwives. One false move, and it's all over. He is the most common type of Man in the Middle, under constant pressure to control his frustration and anger. Not only must he continue to interact with his ex-wife, but he may be paying her spousal or child support (or both) as well, not to mention trying to work through the custody issues. To compound matters, he now has a new woman in his life who also wants his time and attention. And no matter what he does, his problems seem never ending, and his anger continues to mount.

Ex-wives:

- ❧ Keep your interactions with your ex-husband strictly business. Don't try to be his friend or make him your friend; that part of your relationship is over. Stick to the divorce agreement regarding custody and spousal and child support, especially in the beginning. Establishing trust early will lay the foundation for more flexibility in the future.

Stepmothers:

- Be his partner and his friend. Empathize with what he's going through, and don't add to his frustrations by putting undue pressure on him. When you met him, you knew your stepwife would be in the picture. Don't put him in the untenable position of having to placate you when he's simply trying to honor his obligations as a parent. And would you really want to be with a man who would abandon his children?

Men in the Middle:

- You deserve acknowledgment for upholding your end of the commitment you made to take care of your children. We know it often feels as if you are nothing more than a wallet, but that isn't true. Your active presence in your children's lives will prove invaluable to them as they grow and mature into adulthood.

- You need to *remember realistic expectations* when it comes to your ex-wife. You married her, you had children with her, and if you're honest you will admit that there was even a time when you loved her, so she can't be that bad. Moreover, as the mother of your children, you're stuck with her—for better or worse. So treat her with the respect she deserves, and you might just find that she's not that difficult to get along with after all.

❧ You need to be honest with your new wife as to how divided and how torn you feel. Express to her how much you love and need her. Ask for her to understand what you're going through. Be open to her feelings as well.

Once the Tightrope Walker can learn to *talk and communicate effectively* with both stepwives, he may find that the angry, rancorous environment he's living in will begin to dissipate.

The Chameleon

Chuck and Carol had been married for twelve years when they divorced. Several years later, he married Mindy. Not wanting to give up his role as Carol's hero, he remained her confidant, meeting for coffee whenever she needed to talk. When Mindy became upset, he agreed that he should curtail his intimate talks with Carol, but how, without making her upset?

The next type of Man in the Middle owes his name to that fascinating reptile who changes colors depending on *where* he is. Our Chameleon, however, changes depending on *who* he's with. Like the Tightrope Walker, he feels trapped between two women, but rather than being motivated by anger, he is motivated by fear—fear of being the bad guy, fear of losing his children, fear of failing. He tries to keep the peace at all costs and appears to be favoring one or the other stepwife. In order to avoid conflict, the Chameleon tells each stepwife what he thinks they want to hear and then may or may not act on it. The stepmother feels that his loyalties should be to her; she is, after all, his wife. The ex-wife, on the other hand, feels his loyalties should be to her because she is the mother of his children and they have a history together.

Until the Chameleon learns to make the tough call, which will leave someone angry, the potential for conflicts remains high. He can learn to take the risk of not pleasing everyone or can simply throw up his hands in disgust and let the stepwives fend for themselves.

Ex-wives:

✺ Keep your behavior with your ex friendly and civilized, even if you're angry when he doesn't follow through with his promises.

Stepmothers:

✺ He married you, and it's you he loves. Try to empathize with the fact that he is afraid that any conflict with his ex-wife will result in the loss of his children or cost him financially. Help him take small steps toward figuring out a way to talk and communicate effectively with her so everyone can settle into their new roles.

Man in the Middle:

✺ It's important, even imperative, to nurture your new relationship. Take the time to do something special for your wife, the stepmother to your children. It will pay off big-time.

✺ Figuring out how to deal with your ex-wife while at the same time maintaining some distance is a formidable task. *Set limits and boundaries* by letting her know you are willing to *talk and communicate effectively* with her regarding the children. By keeping all interaction to discussions about the kids only, you will reduce the potential conflicts that can so easily arise between exes.

- It's okay (and some would even say a good thing) to have loyalty to the two women, especially since both play such different roles in your life. Loyalty to your wife is expected and appreciated. Loyalty to the mother of your children respects them and the past life you had with their mother.

- We recommend you set up a meeting between you, your new wife, and your ex-wife (and her significant other if appropriate) so each person has the opportunity to voice his or her thoughts. Developing a plan so you can *organize consistently* between both households will allow everyone to feel more comfortable and understand just what their roles are. Children thrive when their parents can *organize consistently,* and never more than when they live in two homes.

- You need to learn some negotiation skills. You are in effect the mediator between the stepwives, and how well you do this job will determine the quality of everyone's life.

If the Chameleon can *set limits and boundaries* with both stepwives, there is a greater chance that peace can prevail in the kingdom.

The I Need a Wife

Bill had always been a workaholic. When he and Jenny divorced, they agreed to joint custody. He, of course, had no idea how he would manage. When he married Sarah, he was more than happy to let her assume much of the responsibility for taking care of his kids, and she was happy to do it. But it didn't take long for her to become completely overwhelmed with her new life as nanny, cook, and chauffeur. To make matters worse, she got no acknowledgment from Jenny, who instead of showing her appreciation for everything Sarah did for her children, simply made everyone's life a living hell.

This man needs a wife, and since his last wife is no longer in the picture, he looks to find someone new—and quickly. If this Man in the Middle isn't careful, he might find himself in the market for wife number three. The I Need a Wife is willing to sacrifice romance for practicality, and when he starts to date again, he will "shop" for someone who can handle his children.

Ex-wives:

- **s** As frustrating as it is, you cannot control what goes on at your ex-husband's house, including what responsibilities your stepwife has assumed regarding your children. Don't be so quick to lay the blame at her feet. She may be playing the "mom role"—carpooling, setting doctors' appointments, and everything else—at the request of her husband. If you feel she's taking over your role, you need to express those concerns.

Stepmothers:

- ❧ It's a tough job trying to balance the many duties you've undertaken in the name of love. You need to *set limits and boundaries* with everyone in your household so they all assume some responsibility in helping you run the house.

Men in the Middle:

- ❧ You married a woman, not a workhorse. She has enormous adjustments to make already. Respect her enough to treat her like the part of your family she is, and acknowledge all she does for you and for everyone. *Remember realistic expectations* regarding her "duties," and bear in mind that they are *your* kids, not hers, and you need to make time for them too.

- ❧ It's completely understandable that you would like your kids and your new wife to be one big happy family right away, but you need to *remember realistic expectations* and give everyone time to get to know each other.

- ❧ Be sure that along with the responsibilities you demand of your wife, you also give her a little authority too. Your children need to know that she is a part of the parenting team. They will respect her role if you allow her to set some rules in your household.

If the I Need a Wife Man in the Middle can *remember realistic expectations,* life at home will be a whole lot easier for everyone.

The Do What I Say or Else

Jesse, one of our radio phone-in callers, had this to say:

I don't want my new wife talkin' to my ex-wife, swappin' stories about me. I never let them talk to each other. I put a block on my ex-wife's phone number so she has no way of calling our house and I don't let my new wife know my ex's number either. I keep 'em apart and that's how I like it. There'll be hell to pay if they ever cross me.

Fortunately the Do What I Say or Else is the least common Man in the Middle we hear about, but he makes the greatest impact on stepwives. He may have a charming exterior but can truly be a wolf in sheep's clothing. Meeting him for the first time, women see him as strong and decisive—a take-charge kind of guy who seems self-assured and treats a woman like a princess. The intensity of his feelings mesmerizes women into believing he possesses great love for them.

The man who starts out looking as if he is determined and in control may be slowly unmasking his underlying craving for power, which is shrouded in his passion and strong will. When he does not get his way, be prepared, because you will be shocked to discover that his fuse is short and the after-effects are serious.

The Do What I Say or Else's behavior can become so inhibiting that stepwives may be forced to keep secrets to avoid the repercussions of even the most innocent of situations. Stepmothers may often feel like prisoners in their own homes, and chances are that his first wife felt the same way. Use the scale we've created to determine the severity of this man's actions:

Normal Behavior	Moderate Problem	Severe Problem	Extreme Problem
Requesting	Critical	Interrogating	Condemning
Raised voice	Screaming	Threatening	Hitting
Compromise	Sometimes compromise	Rarely compromise	Never compromise

Remember that it is normal for a Man in the Middle to be angry and even show it at times. It is not normal, however, when those feelings go beyond the moderate range. If your Man in the Middle falls into the moderate problem range, he has out-of-control tendencies and may be on his way to developing into a full-fledged Do What I Say or Else. Your self-respect is being challenged, so you need a reality check. Join a support group or get counseling. If he falls into the severe problem range, he is damaging to you, the children, and the marriage. Unless he is willing to get help and gain some insight into his actions, your situation will not change. If you were, or are, married to an Extreme Do What I Say or Else, using the PRESCRPTON will not be enough. You must seek help from a professional or law enforcement agency immediately, before harm is done to you or your children. See the resource page.

Golden Rules for the Man in the Middle

We have found that the Man in the Middle can have a positive impact on stepwives by applying the following ten rules:

Keep the door of communication open with your ex-wife as it relates to your children.

Refrain from bad-mouthing your ex-wife.

Be sensitive to your ex-wife's struggle to become financially independent.

Act cordial and respectful to your ex-wife whenever you see her.

Be especially cognizant of the many sacrifices your new wife makes for your children. Express your appreciation to her for all she does for you and your children.

Allow your new wife to have some authority over your children in your house.

Encourage your children to acknowledge their stepmother respectfully.

Work on consistency between the two homes.

Encourage a respectful relationship between the stepwives.

How Skillful Is Your Man in the Middle?

Take the following quiz to find out if your Man in the Middle has the skills he needs to keep peace between the stepwives.

1. When there is a problem between the stepwives, he:
   a. lets them fight it out among themselves.
   b. makes a decision that *puts the kids first.*
   c. files for divorce.
2. When his wife complains that they never go out, he:
   a. tells her his parents never went out.
   b. respects her request and arranges an evening out.
   c. refuses ever to go out again.
3. When his ex-wife tells him her stepwife is taking over her role as mother, he:
   a. pays no attention to her.
   b. *sets limits and boundaries with his wife.*
   c. moves to another town.

4. When his wife tells him that his ex-wife is controlling her life, he:
    a. denies it.
    b. acknowledges her feelings and speaks to his ex-wife.
    c. goes out for a pack of cigarettes and never returns.
5. When his kids tell him they feel torn between the two houses, he:
    a. ignores them.
    b. problem-solves by having an extended-blended family meeting.
    c. takes them to Disneyland.

If you chose *a* for every answer, your Man in the Middle doesn't want to deal with anything and he needs to read this book. If you chose *b* for every answer, your guy is a real negotiator and could run a CoMamas workshop of his own. If you chose *c* for every answer, he is lacking in the skills he needs to be an effective Man in the Middle, but he is definitely not hopeless.

No matter what kind of Man in the Middle you're dealing with, he may not want the stepwives to develop an alliance with each other for a variety of reasons. Perhaps he feels they will exchange unflattering stories about him, affecting his current marriage and lessening his role. Or maybe he just doesn't want his ex-wife in his life any more than necessary—and that's okay. Remember that the goal is for everyone in the extended-blended family to get along in a civilized manner and the Man in the Middle is crucial to making that happen.

The Man on the Outside

> **Our Man on the Outside, Paul:**
>
> *It was a typically beautiful southern California day when Greg and I arrived at Lynne's house to pick up Evan. We were so engrossed in our conversation that we hardly noticed as a man approached the car. He leaned into the car and said, "I figure it's time I met you folks," and I saw Greg reach over to shake the hand of the man who was to become Evan's stepfather.*

The Man on the Outside can be a bit player or star of the show, but he's not really an outsider. He *is* significant and adds one more player to the already overpopulated stepwife relationship. He is the man who surfaces when the ex-wife becomes involved in a relationship or remarries. This usually happens after the ex-husband takes a new wife, but he has been known to appear before that occurs. He may have his own children and ex-wife; thus, our ex-wife may become a stepmother herself.

Men on the Outside have described themselves to us as:

Aloof	Loving	Trusted
Alienated	Unsure	Tired
Friendly	Unaware	Resistant
Different	Hopeful	Popular
Supportive	Stuck	Insignificant

His feelings count, but it's what he does with those feelings that makes a difference in how the Man on the Outside affects the stepwife relationship.

What Kind of Man on the Outside Is He?

Commonly referred to as the stepfather, this man can complicate the stepwife situation by adding his own baggage, or he can help balance it out by promoting peace between the stepwives. Dr. Krausz's experience has helped us to profile the Men on the Outside:

- The White Knight

- The That's Not My Problem

- The Enforcer

The White Knight

> Rhonda and Victor had had a particularly ugly divorce, and although six and a half years had passed, Rhonda was still bitter. When she married Christopher, she thought her life was finally back on track. "Chris and I have a great relationship. He loves me and hates Victor too."

It has been such a long time between men that you were fairly certain it would never happen again—that you would never fall in love. But you have, and he loves everything about you. He thinks you're wonderful and beautiful, and the best mother on the planet, which is a far cry from the treatment you feel you've been receiving from your ex and stepwife. In other words, you can do no wrong. Isn't that a good quality in a man? The answer to that is yes, of course—unless his self-appointed role as your savior begins to provoke the sensitive situation you have with your ex-husband and stepwife.

Sometimes in the White Knight's attempt to support his woman, he fuels fires that are already too hot to begin with by bad-mouthing or blaming *them* for all her problems. It's absolutely appropriate and expected that a Man on the Outside support and side with his wife, but notice we didn't add "at any cost." The White Knight gallops into his wife's world without pulling back on the reins. Although he means to be supportive, he can wind up being intrusive.

Ex-wives:

◆ If you are perpetually complaining about your ex and stepwife, *stop!* This constant pattern gives your new husband the message that you are indeed a victim in need of rescue. Perhaps it's time for you to admit that you still have issues concerning your first marriage to work through.

◆ You need to *set limits and boundaries* with your new husband. Encourage him to allow you to move beyond your anger so you can focus more on your happiness with him and less on what's going on over there.

◆ Reassure him you will respect his opinion even if he doesn't always agree with you.

Men on the Outside:

◆ It's great that you love your woman and support every-thing she stands for, but when it's done in an un-healthy way, you will only further disturb the already precarious predicament she's in. You may need to *claim your own baggage.* Are you behaving this way because you truly believe your wife has been wronged, or do you just want to look good in her eyes no matter what?

❧ By trying to remain objective, you could provide the necessary perspective that is so needed to balance out the stepwife relationship. If you do offer objective advice to your wife, be sure to choose your words carefully so you don't offend her. Try saying "Maybe _____ has a point" versus "I think you're wrong."

The That's Not My Problem

Larry came in upset. It seemed his wife, Sandy, had constant problems with her ex and his new wife. Larry's life had been so much simpler before he married Sandy. He missed his stress-free life and wanted the good times back. Wondering what he had gotten himself into, he was becoming more and more certain the only solution was to leave the marriage.

You thought you had a low-key, laid-back kind of guy, but the That's Not My Problem is anything but that. He stays out of most of his wife's problems with her ex and stepwife—not because he's mellow but because he is afraid of responsibility and conflict.

If he has been married before, you may realize he had a "no-big-deal" attitude and a history of nonparticipation with his own ex and children. After an ex-wife has experienced a traumatic marriage and divorce, the That's Not My Problem's calm persona is attractive, and his real dynamics are overlooked. But no matter what the circumstance sur-rounding this man's entry into an ex-wife's life, it's now time to figure out how to tackle what lies beneath his reluctance to participate.

Ex-wives:

- Now that you've recognized the problem, help him take on more child-rearing responsibilities, one at a time. Go slowly because this is the type of man who will leave if things get too intense.

- *Talk and communicate effectively* with your new hus-band. Maybe he's not participating because he's try-ing to respect your space and your role. Let him know you would like him to be a part of your family and what exactly that means to you.

Men on the Outside:

- You need to face reality. You chose to marry a woman with children, and you are the father figure to those children when they are at your house. So decide what kind of role model you will be and be it; you owe it to the woman you married.

The Enforcer

Patricia was feeling extremely vulnerable when she met Harry, but she was grateful to him for bringing some organization into her life. She began allowing him to do more and more for her and her kids and loved the way he seemed to care about their every thought and feeling. But then his loving interest changed into accusations and inquisitions; her love began to turn to fear, and she didn't know where to turn.

The Enforcer continually crosses the line from being uninvolved and aloof to being abusive—sexually, physically, verbally, or emotionally. Why do women get involved with men like this?

He is distant, which is somewhat mysterious and exciting and can be mistaken for intelligence. A woman who wants to please will work hard to get his undivided attention. He will make demands, and she will succumb. His choices become her choices. His values become her gauge of what is right and wrong. And her self-esteem slowly gets chipped away until there isn't much left.

An early sign of potential abuse is this distant attitude, which is simply his way of ignoring anything that he thinks is insignificant, including his wife's thoughts and feelings. His "suggestions," repeated or hammered in until she finally agrees, are signs of his demanding and controlling personality, which often spills over into his treatment of his stepchildren.

Ex-wives:

ᴥ With this man, the PRESCRPTON will not be enough. Either he agrees to get help, or you get out. The behavior of this type of Man on the Outside will definitely affect your ex-husband and your stepwife, not to mention your children. If you don't tell them yourself,

there is a good chance your children will tell your ex
and stepwife about the frightening situation you're in.

Golden Rules for the Man on the Outside

The Man on the Outside can have a positive influence on
the stepwife relationship by observing the following golden
rules:

Be a good listener for your wife.
Refrain from bad-mouthing her ex or stepwife
Be cordial and respectful to her ex or stepwife during any
  events that involve the children.
Be cognizant of not overstepping your bounds when in-
  teracting with the children.
Encourage consistency between the two homes.
Encourage a respectful relationship between the step-
  wives and with her ex.

Commonly Asked Questions

Stepwives repeatedly ask us how to deal with the men in
their lives. These are their most commonly asked questions:

*What can I do when my ex-husband and new husband
don't get along?* It's hard to believe that men feel the same
competitive urges as women, but if there is a situation that
could bring these feelings out, it is the stepwife scenario.
When you are faced with two men whose hackles are raised
every time they hear about each other, you need to be sensitive to exactly what they're going through. Men are territorial creatures too. And since their feelings can parallel
those of stepwives, the best thing you can do is apply the
PRESCRPTON as you would to your stepwife.

How can I prevent my kids from complaining about their

stepfather to my ex? Often stepfathers feel that as the father figure, they need to apply structure and discipline to stepchildren, who may naturally resent their interference. And who better to complain to than their father? If this is happening in your household, it's time to ask yourself why your child didn't come to you. Along with protecting your child at all costs, you will need to do some damage control with your ex-husband, whose protective paternal instincts have been set into motion after hearing about the stepfather's discipline. A family meeting to uncover what's really going on is in order.

How can I get my ex-husband to treat me with respect? One of the steps of the PRESCRPTON is respect. But if your ex-husband is reluctant to give it to you, don't spend time bemoaning this fact. Respect isn't included in the divorce agreement. Time and distance can be healing, and respect may come back. Consider whether your behavior to him deserves his respect, and always insist that he teach your children to respect you.

When the Man in the Middle and the Man on the Outside provide optimum balance and structure, stepwives will not be left to fend for themselves. You have every right to expect the men in your life to participate, treat you with respect, and protect you with appropriate limits and boundaries. Don't let these two important players in your lives give you anything less.

Chapter 8

Living Arrangements and How to Survive Them

> "Bye, Mom, I love you," said Danny as his mother walked out the door, suitcase in hand. Less than a minute later, Danny answered a loud knock. "Oh, hi, Dad; hi, Melissa," he said greeting his father and stepmother, as their suitcases rolled in through that very same door. "What's for dinner?"

Some of the families we've spoken to have this type of custody arrangement: the kids get the house, and the parents revolve in and out. Of course, this arrangement is unusual. The orchestration of child custody is often much more contentious and can be affected by differing parenting styles and the financial arrangements that go along with them. These two words, *child custody,* are used to describe the living situations dictated by the courts or agreed on by divorcing parents. But *custody* is more than just a legal term defining who gets the children. It includes the responsibilities parents have toward the children, as well as a mandate to act in the child's best interest—or, as we like to say, *put the kids first.*

Coming up with the best possible custody plan is always a challenge, but when a spouse remarries, or asks for increased visitation, stepwives will encounter each other more often.

Until the nineteenth century, children were viewed as

property, and mothers never received custody. But as the industrial revolution forced men from rural homes to factory work in the city and the women's movement gave women and children rights, parenting roles began to change. Women began receiving preference in custody decisions. Decades later, the equal rights movement saw women joining the workforce as men became more involved on the home front. The result is the current trend toward joint custody or shared parenting.[1]

Fathers continue to want to take an active role in the lives of their children after divorce. Many have a bond that is as strong as the mother's, and when they find themselves divorced, they too feel a significant loss in not having their children in their lives on a daily basis. Because most mothers want to retain their roles as well, shared parenting will create tension between the natural parents and stepwives. We know shared parenting can bring heartache, but if stepwives can learn to get along, they can provide the children with the next best thing to having Mom and Dad together: an extended-blended family who loves and cares for them. This doesn't mean shared parenting works for everyone, and there are some circumstances when this living arrangement is not recommended:

- ❧ Severe and crippling addiction in the family

- ❧ A history of reported family violence

- ❧ Diagnosed but untreated mental illness in one of the parents or stepparents

Life in an extended-blended family is not easy even in the best of situations. Everyone needs to make adjustments, no matter what type of custody model they choose, because the lives of children are at stake. Whatever type of custody arrangement you're involved in, you should *expect* problems, but there is a way we can help you cut them down to a manageable size.

Custody Models

There are many types of custody models, each with its own accompanying problems. Even when parents make arrangements without intervention from the courts, it is almost impossible to avoid disagreements between households. These are the three most common types of custody models we see:

- Sole custody

- 80/20 custody

- 50/50 custody

Sole Custody

John left shortly after Tyler was born, and Allison thought they'd never hear from him again. When he and his new wife called to invite Tyler to come for a visit, Allison grudgingly let him go. Returning home, Tyler remarked, "I had fun with my dad, and my new mother is really nice. Can I go again?" Over my dead body, thought Allison.

If you are the biological mother (or father, for that matter), you might feel relief that you have been granted sole custody. Now you won't have to deal with your ex and his new spouse. So then what's the problem? The problem is your child has only one of his parents in his life, and in most situations this is not always beneficial for the child.

Whether sole custody includes visitation, supervised or unsupervised, is a matter decided by the court. Supervised visitation is usually decreed when one parent is declared unfit. Unsupervised visitation means that the parent is capable of being with the child on his own but may not be able to care for the child for extended periods of time. And some parents have sole custody because the other parent has simply left, never to be heard from again.

No matter what the circumstances surrounding sole custody, your children will be curious about their other parent. Talk to the children, stressing the positive qualities of that parent. Don't deny them the opportunity to learn about their mom or dad. Encourage communication between the children and the parent they don't see.

Ex-wives:

- If you have sole custody of your son, contact an agency such as the Big Brothers of America so your child can have a male role model in his life. Statistics prove overwhelmingly that boys especially need a father figure.

Stepmothers:

- Encourage your husband to reach out to his children. They need each other, and he has a financial as well as emotional responsibility to the children he fathered.

To address the difficulties in divorce, David L. Levy, president and co-founder of the Children's Rights Council, petitioned Congress in 1985 to provide the first ever federal funding for programs to connect children to their noncustodial parents. This funding was part of the Family Support Act, which became federal law in 1988. The Children's Rights Council, a national child advocacy organization with chapters in most states, operates more than twenty transfer sites for children, usually in church day care centers. These sites allow parents to transfer their children peacefully from one parent to the other and thereby avoid the acrimony that often occurs when parents are separated, divorced, or never married. CRC also runs more than five supervised access sites. (For more information about CRC, see the Resources Section.)

80/20 Custody

Five-year-old Cory hyperventilated every time his mom took him on the plane to visit his dad. After the doctors said there was nothing wrong with him, his mom brought him to us. As it turned out, Cory felt anxious because he didn't know what he was "supposed to do" when he was with his father. We developed a plan for his dad to call him more often and specifically talk about a schedule for the upcoming visit. Cory felt better just knowing what to expect.

Although this is not the only formula for unequal shared parenting, it is the most common, and it is usually the mother who has the children 80 percent of the time. Typically, the children visit the Dad's house every other weekend and two extra nights a month, unless the mom and dad live in different cities. In this case, the kids visit during winter, summer, and spring breaks. Either way, the mom's house becomes the home base, where homework is done, chores are assigned, and a consistent bedtime is strictly observed. The stress created by the mother's one-parent lifestyle may cause her to be impatient. In the less frequent case where the situation is reversed and the father has 80 percent custody and has remarried, the stress placed on the stepmother may be even greater. It's time for both woman to nurture themselves and maybe even try to help each other out.

Whether or not you live in the same town, we recommend that the noncustodial parent communicate frequently with their child. Send e-mails, pictures, videos, and cards, and schedule phone conversations, especially when a visit is imminent. Resist the urge to be a Disneyland parent. Children need to see their parents as more than just providers of fun and games. Get to know your children and let them get to know you. It's okay to relax with your kids without having to entertain them.

Children feel anxiety when they visit a parent they haven't seen in a long time, even if they speak to the parent regularly. They need to have as much consistency when they "visit" as they do when they're "at home." When you do your scheduling, be sure everyone has their share of long weekends, holidays, and family birthdays. Develop your own rituals or traditions so each child will feel special at your house.

Stepmothers:

- If you and your husband are the noncustodial parents, you may feel like a third wheel or persona non grata when your husband spends time with his kids. Let your spouse know you would like to spend some time with him *and* his children, yet don't forget to respect his time alone with them.

❧ If you feel left out when your husband is with his kids, use this time to nurture your relationships with your own family.

50/50 Custody

> *When my ex left me for another woman, our son was only eighteen months old. I was completely devastated and of course didn't want her anywhere near my son. My ex and I ended up in court and spent thousands of dollars, only to end up with joint custody, which I fought. Now, though, I'm really happy because I actually have some time for myself, which I would never have had if I had gotten full custody. And when I'm with my son, I can give him real quality time.*

When the custody arrangement is a 50/50 split, the stepwife relationship can get intense—fast! You can no longer put off making peace with your stepwife. Stay positive. The biggest plus of all is that the children have a chance to have both parents participate in their lives. Fifty/fifty custody also allows each set of parents a better understanding of the actual costs of raising children, which will hopefully diminish the accusations and blaming that usually go along with divorce and remarriage.[2]

It helps to *organize consistently* and develop a specific calendar in this type of custody arrangement so that the children know ahead of time where they'll be. Including the children in the planning will make them feel more secure about their divided life in two households. Once the calendar is in place, it needs to be reviewed periodically as everyone's needs grow and change.

Survival Techniques

Whichever custody plan you have, the following techniques will help things run more smoothly for you as you implement your plan:

- *Care* enough about the children to do your homework. Understand their needs based on their age, personality, and emotionality. Think about a variety of different ways you can raise them to be healthy adults.

- *Create* a plan for *organizing consistently* that fits the specific needs of the children, not what is convenient for you as parents.

- *Communicate* in a way that allows you to *empathize and acknowledge* the feelings of your stepwife, ex, and spouse. Imagine yourself sharing your thoughts and ideas, as well as listening to the other person. Communication is key to problem solving and must be ongoing.

- *Collaborate* by keeping yourself open to finding the middle ground in which to work. Remind yourself that no one is all right or all wrong. *Putting the kids first* means letting go of some of your control.

- *Cooperate* with each other over and over until it becomes second nature.

Put It on Paper

> *Because my mom hated my stepmom and they had different rules at each house, I learned to play one house against the other to get whatever I wanted. I became extremely manipulative, and now, as an adult, I can't have a healthy relationship with anyone. I wish they had learned to work together.*

We have designed the Extended-Blended Family Form to help you organize between the two households. (You will find it in the Resources section at the back of the book.) Remember that what you do now can affect your children's lives for many years to come.

You will need at least one meeting or phone call to complete the Extended-Blended Family Form. Tackle the simpler topics first, and then move on to the tougher ones. And remember this form is not set in stone. Revise the form as needed.

Keep these points in mind as you fill out the form:

❧ Scheduling specific days and times when the kids can call the other parent will help them feel more in control of their environment.

❧ When dropping the children off or picking them up, choose a consistent but neutral spot. If you plan to deliver them to the other parent's house, call ahead and drop them off in the driveway. Have the child signal you by flicking the porch light or calling your cell phone so you know he arrived inside safely.

✥ Do not schedule appointments (doctor, dentist, hair cut) or set up regular activities (soccer, music lessons) during the other household's recognized custody time. If it is unavoidable, call to check with them first. You don't want anyone scheduling something during your week, so reciprocate in kind.

✥ Work together to help each child reach his or her potential, whether it means paying for a tutor, private school, college, or extracurricular activities. *Put the kids first,* and don't let them be the target of your ongoing anger with each other.

✥ Have a list of the child's doctors and medical insurance information in case of emergency. If you're going to be away, ask the other parent if he would like the opportunity to be with the kids during this time. Make sure the other household has a number where you can be reached, even if you feel your whereabouts are none of their business.

In addition to the Extended-Blended Family Form, you can also integrate the What's Happening Form (also in the Resources section) into your life. This important aid can keep miscommunications to a minimum. By filling out this form and hand-delivering, faxing, or placing it in your child's backpack, you will be giving your stepwife important information that she needs to have about the child.

Even when you use the What's Happening and the Extended-Blended Family forms, we have found it is difficult to have a harmonious shared custody situation without knowing something about parenting styles. Many of the disagreements that are part of shared custody stem from arguments over whose way is the best way to parent.

Parenting Styles

When the parenting styles of the two stepwives are dramatically different, you can be sure there will be conflict. Within an intact family, one parent generally falls into the role of nurturer, while the other is more of an authority figure. But when families break up, roles change; they have to. And when the families are reconstituted, each house may take on the style of the biological parent.

If the biological parenting styles were different to begin with, they may now be worlds apart, causing stepwives to judge each other relentlessly. Your perceptions may be a little skewed, so be careful not to exaggerate your stepwife's parenting style. And ex-wives shouldn't assume that the relationship they had with their ex is necessarily the same as the one he has with their children.

Ask any stepwife, and she'll tell you that one of the most difficult aspects of sharing custody is the different parenting styles at both houses—with each parent feeling his or her approach is the best for the child. Even when stepwives have similar values, how they choose to teach them is another story. When methods of raising children are poles apart or are inconsistent even within the same household, the children, stepwives, and the Man in the Middle and Man on the Outside will certainly be confused, frustrated, and angry.

In her practice, Dr. Krausz has seen many different parenting styles and finds that some parents have no consistent style at all, which can confuse the children and stepwives alike. These are the styles she sees most frequently:

- ◈ My Way Or No Way

- ◈ Free-for-All

- ◈ Fair But Not Equal

My Way or No Way

> *Tricia brought seven-year-old Crystal in to see us because she was concerned over her need to fold her clothes over and over again. At first, Tricia thought it was cute and even helpful, until Crystal started sorting everything in sight. Then she noticed that each time Crystal returned from visiting her dad, whom Tricia had divorced because of his overbearing and rigid behavior, her daughter's obsessive tendencies seemed to get worse.*

Open discussion and exchange of ideas are not options with the My Way or No Way. Their word is law, and they discipline through blatant intimidation or more passive, nonverbal approaches. The My Way or No Way parent uses tactics that involve control, rigidity, and intolerance. Children respond to this type of parent in several ways: anxiety, fear, escape, or revenge. A child who is anxious feels out of control inside. Feeling uncomfortable, it is not uncommon for many children to attempt to control their environment by exhibiting obsessive thoughts and actions (e.g., constant organizing, cleaning, sorting, or perseverating on a particular subject.)

When children feel as though they are in a no-win situation, some become withdrawn and depressed. Daydreaming, long periods of silence, and choosing to play alone are some examples. Finally, there are those children who learn another frightening lesson: intimidation gives one the upper hand and control in any situation.

Free-for-All

Helen, her ex, and her stepwife agreed that their son, Roger, would not get his driver's license until he was seventeen due to his poor grades. This was a big step because Helen had always thought that her ex and stepwife were too lenient with Roger. Unbeknownst to her, the rules changed when her ex and stepwife moved farther away from the high school. No longer wanting to drive him to school every day, they took Roger to get his license and bought him a car without consulting Helen.

Anything goes with these classic permissive parents. Whether they feel guilty for working too much, aren't spending enough time with the children, or are fearful that the children won't love or accept them, they create an atmosphere of few rules and little to no consequences. Being too lax in parenting creates an environment with no structure or boundaries. By not providing a healthy set of rules, these parents are not giving their children a strong foundation based on important values. How can anyone who is able to get away with just about anything have a sense of what is right or wrong? The end result is that children will push both stepwives to their limits and beyond, as they cry out for consistency and respectful perimeters.

Fair But Not Equal Parent

When parenting, the Fair But Not Equal takes into account a child's age, personality, and the various emotional, social, and developmental levels that are unique to each child. Although these parents have common rules and values, they are open to different ways of teaching. No matter what approach they use, this parent teaches and practices respect through consistent communication and actions. The outcome of this consistent approach is that the children are able to trust the most important people in their lives and will have the confidence to make sound decisions and have strong relationships. When children have structure in their lives, they learn about responsibilities and consequences. These children are then able to stay focused, set goals, and, most important, know they are loved unconditionally. This is the parenting style we are all hoping to achieve.

How to Find the Middle Ground

One of the most common complaints we hear from stepwives is how their different parenting styles wreak havoc in their lives. Whether it's an ex-wife complaining that her stepwife is too hard on her children or a stepmother complaining that the ex-wife is too permissive, take heart; there is a solution. We have successfully helped many stepwives find the middle ground where compromise reigns supreme, whether they work at it independently or together.

Stepwives who are interested in meeting to discuss their different styles of parenting are off to a good start. Before the meeting, each should write down the values they feel are important for the children. Because anxieties of stepwives who are meeting run so high, it is always important to prepare ahead so nothing will be overlooked. Here's how to get started:

- Describe your particular type of parenting style. You may find that you have elements from all three styles.

Pick the style in which the majority of your characteristics are represented.

⊷ Describe the special qualities of each child. This
will help you tailor your teaching to the child's
individual strengths and weaknesses. If your child ex-
cels at sports, for instance, use this venue to teach
cooperation, hard work, and the merits of follow-
through.

⊷ Write down your goals and concerns for your child.
Think about long-range goals first. What kind of person do you want your child to be? What would you like
your child to accomplish now and or in five or ten
years?

⊷ Prioritize your goals and concerns. Rank these in as-
cending order, with your most important goals first,
your least important last. Decide how you will teach
them.

The Meeting

If you need to brush up on the protocol for meeting with
your stepwife, refer to Chapter 6. Then proceed:

1. Look for some commonality in your lists. Many people
   find that their top priorities are actually quite similar
   (honesty, integrity, respect for elders) and that their
   goals and concerns are in sync on high-priority items.
2. Pick the top three areas, and brainstorm ways you can be
   consistent in implementing the goals with the children.
   If you both feel honesty is important, you will want to
   provide honest role models and reward your children

when they are honest. You can read books and stories with morals emphasizing the value of honesty. Be creative.

4. Identify the discrepancies in your styles and how that may affect the children. If one household requires the children to make their beds before school and the other doesn't, keep things in perspective. What is the worst that will result from this discrepancy?

5. It is impossible for you to be aligned on every issue, so you need to pick your battles and focus on the high-priority items—in other words, don't sweat the small stuff.

Deidra found that by repeatedly asking her mom and stepmom to do things for her, she would ultimately get her way. Both stepwives met to discuss this problem and claimed their own baggage. They realized that they had participated in teaching Deidra to manipulate both of them early on. Deciding to set limits and boundaries with Deidra, they agreed to check with each other before responding to Deidra's requests.

When You Have to Go It Alone

When you are not on speaking terms with your stepwife, try the following:

1. Write down the values that you want to teach the children. Stick with only ten items, and prioritize them in order of importance.

2. Describe the personalities of the children. If your child is withdrawn, you will want to take a different approach than you would if he were angry and hostile. Good par-

enting involves taking personality traits into consideration.

3. What are your concerns regarding their upbringing? Are
   they living with inconsistencies? Poor role models? Bad-
   mouthing? Prioritize these in terms of their importance
   to you.

4. Write down your goals for each child. If you value and
   want your children to have an exceptional education,
   begin working on this goal early. Schedule trips to the library, museum, and historic landmarks. Implement a
   plan that includes study in a quiet place at the same time
   each day. Be certain to check their homework when it's
   completed.

5. Write down the positive aspects of your stepwife's parenting style (e.g., she prepares special meals for her children; they roller-skate together). Now put yourself in
   your stepwife's shoes. Answer questions 1-4 again, only
   imagine you are she. What values do you think are important to her? Does she see the kids the same way you
   do? How is she teaching the children values?

6. What similarities and differences in your parenting
   styles do you see? Are your styles very different? Who is
   more flexible? More consistent?

> *When Basia went through the exercise above at one of
> our workshops, she was surprised that her stepwife, Leti-
> cia, really was a good mom. She had always looked at
> Leticia's roller-skating with the kids as a sign of her im-
> maturity. But when she stepped into Leticia's shoes, she
> realized that the roller-skating was really an effective
> way for the children to spend quality time with their
> mother. Doing this reality check helped Basia diffuse*

some of her anger and become less critical of Leticia's parenting style.

He Lets Me Drive But Not Discipline

Some stepmothers tell us their husbands don't permit them to discipline the children, or if they are allowed to take on a disciplinary role, they find themselves continually undermined by their husband. What can you do if you are a stepmother who finds herself in this position?

1. Write down the positive and negative aspects of your parenting as a couple. Be specific. Perhaps you are a screamer and he is more easy-going, or he gives consistent consequences to help teach new behaviors when you feel just talking is enough.
2. Communicate with your spouse regarding your feelings and concerns about the differences in your styles and what you're teaching the kids. Use your "I" statements and remember that they are his children, not yours.
3. Brainstorm ways you can be consistent in teaching the children the values that are important to each of you. You are both on the same team—the one rooting for his kids—so it shouldn't be that difficult to come to a compromise.
4. If your spouse doesn't want your participation in disciplining the children because he is afraid of "losing them" or that they will not love him, address this concern lovingly. Not setting limits and boundaries with the children teaches them disrespect not only toward the stepmother but toward their father as well.
5. If you find that your techniques are too different, read a parenting book (see the Resources section) or take a par-

enting class together. Whether your child is a toddler or an adolescent, it's never too late to learn good parenting skills.

If you complete these exercises and find you are still having difficulty overcoming the differences in your parenting styles, perhaps your expectations as a parent are unrealistic. Consult the following positive parenting practices to see if your parenting skills are on track:

Give children love and praise. Praise encourages children to repeat positive behavior.

Listen to your children. Listening carefully helps you learn about your children.

Understand your children. Understanding prepares you to deal effectively with your children's needs.

Set limits. The family needs limits on time, boundaries, and behaviors.

Encourage independence. Understanding limits helps children set their own.

Promote responsibility. Be sure children complete tasks from beginning to end.

Discuss emotions. Allow children to express themselves, and let them know your feelings.

Model good examples. Children learn from watching others.

No matter what situation you're in, it is extremely important to find the middle ground because children can so easily play parents against each other or things can slip through the cracks, especially when both biological parents no longer live in the same house. When stepwives accept what the kids say about what goes on at the other house as gospel, without giving the benefit of the doubt to their step-wife, misinterpretations and misunderstandings arise.

Stepwives:

- Rules and consequences for breaking them should go with the children no matter whose house they're in. If the children know that certain behaviors (lying, stealing, talking back) won't be tolerated at either house and that each household will follow though with consequences, any differences in parenting styles will be minimized.

- Control your impulse to rescue the children from the other house when you hear their other parent isn't being fair. Make sure you clarify the situation with your stepwife so you know the facts.

Most of the disagreements you and your stepwife will have will be related to the different parenting styles you each use to reach your goals and not necessarily the goals themselves.

Financial Wars

Carlos was CEO of a large company and lived in a beautiful house complete with pool and tennis courts—until the divorce. His ex-wife, Amy, got herself a top-notch attorney, and when they were done with Carlos, he and his new wife, Brenda, were barely able to afford a home of their own. Brenda became so bitter and resentful that she filed for divorce, leaving Carlos and Amy's children devastated. Now they were the victims of two broken homes.

Money and finances play a significant role after divorce. Financial wars create explosive emotional and psychological problems, and it's no surprise that exes can be tied up in court for years. Just the word *money* brings out the worst in stepwives. No matter who has more, money will create power plays in the stepwife relationship.

Some statistics estimate that divorced women have close to a 40 percent decrease in their standard of living after divorce. This might explain why some women push for sole custody: they get more money. With money representing power, happiness, security, control, dependency, independence, freedom, and more, it's not surprising how it affects divorces and stepwife relationships.[3] Advocates for shared parenting, however, state that joint custody enhances the child's financial position and encourages voluntary payment of child support.[4] The amount of spousal and child support depends on the laws of the state and several other important factors

Spousal support is considered when:

- ☙ The marriage was long term, usually fifteen years or longer.

- ☙ The ex-wife was a stay-at-home mom most of her marital years.

- ☙ The ex-wife has few skills, is unemployable, or is incapacitated by illness.

- ☙ The husband makes a lot of money or has the potential of high earnings.

Spousal support often stops when the ex-wife remarries, the last child is out of the house, or the ex-wife develops new skills or completes her education to make herself employable.[5] Fewer women are being awarded spousal support now that so many women work outside the home.

Child custody and support are emotional issues for step-wives. How much a parent pays in child support creates a built-in litigious relationship among all the parents. The more one parent has the child, the less the other wants to pay in child support. The courts look closely at what's in the child's best interest by considering the following factors in determining child support:

- Parents' income

- Amount of time each parent has the child

- Number of children and their ages

- Special needs or health issues of the child

Other factors considered are medical insurance, housing, and activities the child is involved in.[6] Although there isn't one specific formula to determine child support, the following is an example of one that is commonly used:

Mother's income = $20,000
Father's income = $45,000
Combined income = $65,000

The mother's share of the combined income is $20,000 divided by $65,000 or 31 percent. The father's share of the combined income is $45,000 divided by $65,000, or 69 percent. Therefore, the father pays 69 percent of the child support, and the mother is responsible for 31 percent.

Stepwives as Paupers

You wake up one morning and realize you're alone and you've lost almost half of your financial position. Yet you still need to pay the rent, clothe your children, and eat. And you notice that your ex and stepwife just bought themselves a second home. Even with your spousal and child support and weekly paycheck, you still find yourself coming up short, and you are furious. Why does *she* get the expensive perks while you have to pinch every penny? Did your husband pull a fast one on you, or are you overreacting?

Having financial problems adds stress and strain to any divorce and marriage. No matter how angry you are, keeping yourself in the victim role regarding your financial situation will not help change the circumstances. Being proactive in the solution will bring more positive results for you and the children. Although the following suggestions are not cure-alls, they attempt to help you look at your financial state of affairs with an objective pair of eyes.

Ex-wives:

- •s Reevaluate your job skills and job opportunities. Earning extra money through odd jobs can help on a short-term basis, but you need to have a long-term plan to be financially stable. And no matter what your ex is contributing, you need to be prepared for the day your child support comes to an end.

- •s Take out a loan or borrow money from a friend or financial institution, perhaps to finish your education or earn a vocational degree.

❧ Make an alteration in your living arrangements. Move in with a friend or relative who is in the same situation, or get a boarder to help you offset your rent.

As always, there is a flip side to everything, and the money situation is no exception. If you've married a man who has suffered a financial setback due to his divorce, you may feel a little like a sacrificial lamb. First, you sacrificed your dream of a perfect marriage by marrying a man with children, then you took on the responsibilities of helping care for them, and now you're being asked to give up those little niceties you feel entitled to and his ex-wife is still enjoying. And you resent the hell out of her for it.

From the CoMamas Web site:

I want out of my marriage. My husband gives in to anything his ex-wife wants, and I'm sick of it. I love my stepchildren and have always contributed financially, but I'm tired of sacrificing for them. There is never any money left over for us, and I don't want to live this way anymore.

Stepmothers:

❧ We know how difficult it is to give up so much and feel as if you're receiving so little. Go to the place inside yourself where the most adult "you" resides, and remind yourself what life was like as a single woman. Now think about all the ways your life has been enhanced by your husband and his children.

❧ Cultivate positive feelings toward your stepchildren by including them in activities you enjoy. When you love and appreciate your stepchildren, it won't feel quite so bad to give to them rather than yourself. The more you value your relationship with your husband and stepchildren, the less you will feel as if you are at the bottom of the financial food chain.

- ⚜ Consider joining a barter club where you can exchange services. For example, if you are a hair stylist, you may do someone's hair in exchange for goods and services that you need that the client can provide.

- ⚜ Find ways of economizing on the home front. Be creative: bargain-shop, clip coupons, and scour the town for the many discounts available.

Deadbeat Dads

When the ex-husband is involved with his child and feels a part of that child's life, he will be more likely to contribute and meet his financial responsibility. Most women say the reason they are not receiving payment is that their ex is unemployed, angry with them, or doesn't manage his money well.[7]

If the ex-husband is still furious with his ex-wife and doesn't send his check on time, he is not only asking for trouble; he puts his kids at risk. When an ex-wife is dependent on this money to support herself and the children, she will be forced to fight any way she can for survival. Feeling desperate and powerless, she may engage in bad-mouthing and other destructive behaviors that can easily affect her stepwife, whom she may blame for diverting her rightful funds.

It's not always the man who has to pay child and spousal support. Although six times more women than men receive spousal and child support,[8] it doesn't make it any easier to swallow for the small but growing number of women who end up footing the bill for the marriage gone awry. Imagine what this does to the stepwife relationship.

Commonly Asked Questions

Every stepwife needs to know how to solve the problems intrinsic to custody, parenting styles, and finances. We get the following questions most frequently:

How can we talk about money without fighting? Besides custody, money is one of the most volatile subjects stepwives deal with. Money symbolizes different things for everyone. Set goals about what you want for your children's future, and work toward those goals together. You may want to contact a mediator or financial planner if you have difficulty focusing on the children's needs rather than your own.

How can I get my child support without putting my kid in the middle? Every time you ask your children to get money from their father, they are thrown into the middle of your financial war. Try communicating with your ex as to how the financial situation is affecting the child. Use your "I" statements and what is commonly referred to as the "sandwich" approach:

1. Start with a positive comment or compliment.
2. Address your concern respectfully.
3. Use an open-ended question to encourage discussion.
4. End with a positive comment or compliment—for example, "I know you're working very hard and trying your best to take care of the children, whether they are with you or with me. However, when I don't receive their check on time, it makes it hard to get everything they need. What are some other ways you can think of to ensure that

the check arrives on time? . . . I appreciate some of the points you brought up."

You may want to offer some alternatives, such as paying twice a month rather than once, or a portion from each paycheck. There is nothing more polarizing than finding yourself in front of a judge, paying enormous attorneys' fees and dragging your children through the mud one more time. Repeated court battles take you away from what should be your ultimate goal: figuring out how to work together as members of the same parenting team.

Chapter 9

The Kids: POWs or Respected Dignitaries?

Evan's story:

> To most people, my situation may look a little weird, trapped between two people who want to make decisions for me and about me. To me, however, this is everyday life, and I hardly give it a second thought, I don't think that this whole "conflict" over me has affected me too much. Mom and Weese, for the most part, kept me in the dark about all the squabbles.
>
> Although I realized fairly early on that they would never be friends, I had no idea about what was really going on. Some of the events in this book come as a shock to me, while others I did have some idea about. I pretty much avoided trying to get involved in their talks, leaving them to handle the situations like civilized (I use the term loosely) adults. Every now and then, one of them would say "Would you ask X if you can spend the weekend with us? We are going to visit Y and would like you to come." I would usually respond by asking them why they didn't do it themselves instead.
>
> At some events where they all met together, I could tell there was obvious tension and sometimes felt slight embarrassment at having a whole entourage with me. I guess it was lucky for me they didn't get along and therefore didn't get into these situations too much. I really

don't mind so much anymore. Sometimes I feel almost of-
fended when they don't all show up . . . sometimes.

I can remember from time to time hearing one of them
complaining about the other behind closed doors, but I
mostly ignored it. Then my world changed. They decided
to write this book. I can only imagine it as something sim-
ilar to the fall of the U.S.S.R. (I don't really remember it
too well), but all the long-held ideologies turn topsy-turvy
and enemies become friends.

I imagine this endeavor will probably benefit their re-
lationship. It has made my life much, much easier. They
are spending more time on the phone talking to each other
than I do talking to them. What a difference a day makes.

The kids. Without them, this book would never have been
written. In fact, most stepwives would agree that without
the kids, they would have no reason ever to be in contact
with each other.

We know it's hard to put up a front for the children when
your emotions are completely out of whack, but remember
that your role as a parent mandates protecting your children. You need to think clearly about what is important to
their well-being. Young children believe that their parents
can do no wrong. Look back on your own childhood and
think about how invincible you thought your parents were,
no matter how they behaved. If you do not behave like an
adult, your kids will surely suffer.

It doesn't matter how long you've been divorced from
their father or been their stepmother; it's time for you both
to get past previous difficulties. Your (step)children are
yearning for structure and consistency, yet after divorce
and remarriage, what they get is a world full of fighting and

chaos, where adults behave more like children than grown-ups, a world in which children are treated like prisoners of war instead of the respected dignitaries they are entitled to be.

As they try to make sense of the shattered world in which they've been put, kids are often plagued by complex emotions, which they may be unable to express. Use shadow talk to prompt a discussion of your children's feelings. "If I were you, I might feel worried or scared that when Daddy remarries, you won't see me very often. Are you feeling worried or scared?" or "I understand that many children feel confused when they have two houses to live in. Do you feel that way sometimes?"

Become acquainted with the typical emotions children feel after divorce and remarriage, and keep them in mind when interacting with the children:

Confusion	Anger	Depression
Worry	Anxiety	Sadness
Guilt	Fear	Displaced
Loss	Vulnerable	Unprotected
Unloved	Neglected	Worthless

If your children display any of these emotions, try to get them to talk about their feelings because if they are not able to share their feelings, they will either bottle them up or act them out. The outcome of helping children understand and express their feelings is that they will be able to cope more effectively in the confusing, changing world of divorce and remarriage. Validating and encouraging appropriate ways of expressing feelings helps children feel more confident in communicating them when other situations come up in their lives that are stressful or even joyful.

Stuck in the Middle

> *"Why don't I get to see my daddy anymore?" David asked his mother, Katrina. "Doesn't he still love me?" "You're not going to see your father ever again until he pays me what he owes me!" screamed Katrina. "But I miss my daddy," David said, his lip quivering as he began to cry. "Well, if he really loved you, he'd pay me what he owes me."*

We can't emphasize enough how important it is to separate your issues from the child's issues. "Child" issues have to do with the well-being of children—how they feel and what is important to them. "Adult" issues have to do with your own feelings about your situation. Keep the kids out of the middle. Adults who continually confuse these issues rob their children of their childhood. An example of this occurs every time a child says, "When can I see my daddy? I miss him," and the mother responds, "Not until he pays me the child support he owes me." If these words sound familiar, it's never too late to change.

When children are older and understand the value of money, parents can discuss some financial situations with them. The maturity of the child and the reason for the discussion dictate the information that can be discussed. Teaching them that you are living on a budget and sharing relevant information and rules regarding your own household financial situation is fine. It's when a parent badmouths the other parent for holding back funds or wants to use money as a weapon in a custody battle that those discussions become inappropriate to have with the children. Here are some suggestions that have helped others in your situation begin to transform their POWs into respected dignitaries:

Stepwives:

❧ Think about how you contributed to their feeling like POWs. Have you bad-mouthed your stepwife or their father in front of them? Have you discussed financial conflicts with or in front of them?

❧ Determine what part your stepwife and your ex are playing in the difficulty. This should be done without laying blame on each other.

❧ Before you tell the children anything about what is going on in your life, ask yourself how they will benefit from this information. If the answer is *not at all*, bite your lip and walk away.

You're Not My Mother

Ellen's stepchildren refused to do anything around the house. "They act like this is a hotel and I'm the innkeeper!" Her feelings of being taken for granted continued until she found herself constantly screaming at everyone, including her husband. She was at her wit's end when she came to see us.

"I don't have to listen to you." Almost every stepmother has heard these words in one form or another. If she hasn't heard them, she's probably experienced the hostile or passive behavior that usually accompanies them.

It's difficult enough for kids to adjust to their parents' divorce, but add stepparents, living in two homes, and new siblings, and it may be too much for a child to take. Children have no idea why their parents couldn't work out their problems. It wasn't their choice for their parents to be unhappy and divorce or to have a stepmother enter their lives. Many times children don't even know that their parents are unhappy and may be completely shocked to hear the news about the divorce.

So what do they do? Consciously or unconsciously, children may try to reunite their parents by creating conflicts with their stepmother and, like the ex-wife, try to regain control over a life that feels as if its spiraling out of control. And who better to take the brunt of all that anger and confusion than their stepmother?

Fortunately, we've heard from stepmothers everywhere who truly love their stepchildren and are loved by them in return. However, if you find yourself in a situation where anger is the rule rather than the exception, do the following:

Stepmothers:

❦ Let your stepchildren know that you feel their mother is a wonderful person, even if you are stretching the truth, and that you're not trying to replace her. Respecting their feelings about their mother in this manner will go a long way toward gaining their trust.

❦ Have a family meeting to *talk and communicate effectively* about the expectations you have for them when they're with you. Work into the disciplinary role gradually to allow them the time they need to adjust to your presence.

You Don't Like His Kids, and They Don't Like You

Even if you're doing your very best to find your place as a stepmother, sometimes the children just won't like you and you're not sure why. Here are some answers:

- They believe that as long as their parents are single, they may get back together. It's every child's dream to have a happy, intact family. They long for a mom and dad who love each other and them, have dinner together, go on vacations, and share holidays and special events. It's what feels normal, and children need to feel normal. You represent the end of that dream.

- They feel protective of their mother, especially if she's single. They may feel disloyal if they participate in a family with you while their mother is alone. Struggling with these feelings often causes children to act out and behave badly.

- They may feel you are trying to replace their mother, and they are letting you know in no uncertain terms that you are *not* their mother. They feel as though you are taking their father's time and attention away from them. They have already lost their family structure and have had to adjust to a whole new way of life. Competing with you for their father's attention compounds the feelings of confusion and uncertainty they may be having.

On the other hand, you may not like your stepchildren and may not be sure why. Here are some possibilities:

❧ You fell in love with a guy and didn't want to think about anything marring that happiness. You didn't like his kids from the start, but chances are you thought you just might grow to love them. It never happened.

❧ You are jealous of the relationship they have with their dad. Although you knew he had kids and saw them regularly, you didn't anticipate that you would continue feeling like such an outsider.

❧ You don't like the way they treat you. Although you understand that their treatment of you is the result of the pain and confusion they feel at not having their parents together, you just can't tolerate being treated like a nonperson.

Children are already the victims in the dissolution of their parent's marriage and have experienced a great loss. Imagine they are children of a friend or a relative. Would you view the situation differently? Would you expect them to feel pain and confusion? Would you want to protect them from further pain? If the answer is yes, consider transferring these feelings to your stepchildren and see if you can get past their dislike of you or your dislike of them and become a positive influence in their lives.

My Mom Needs Me

An ex-wife has to add actress to her list of duties if she wants to prevent her children from realizing how hard it is on her when their father remarries. Many single mothers and even fathers, after all the loss they've sustained, believe that their children are the only ones still in their corner and lean on them for emotional support. Once the stepmother becomes part of the family unit and the father's marital status changes, it is typically the mother who is guilty of leaning too hard on her children. All too often, young children become the keepers of their mother's anxieties over financial, emotional, and career difficulties and decisions, leaving the children little to no room to deal with their own worries and fears.

When you feel your children are your only source of comfort or emotional security, you set yourself up to be upset when they show love toward and accept their stepmother. When you don't protect your children from your feelings of replacement and jealousy, they can suffer serious loyalty conflicts. Afraid of hurting you, they often feel pressured to reject their stepmother. Or if they do accept her anyway, they risk their own mother's seeing them as traitors. Your innocent children find themselves stuck in an emotional trap that you have set for them. Ensure that your children won't be caught in this trap.

Ex-wives:

- Keep adult issues to yourself. If you feel you have no one to confide in, join a support group.

- Use the problem-solving strategy in Chapter 2 so you can systematically solve your own problems.

- *Nurture yourself* when your kids are at their dad's. Do something you wouldn't normally have an opportunity to do when the kids are around. Join a book club, or go to dinner with friends. Use this time to recharge so you can be stronger when they return.

Knowing that their mother feels afraid and unable to handle her life makes children feel insecure, so keep in mind that your children are not your confidants or possessions and that their purpose isn't to prop you up emotionally.

Bad-mouthing

Candace shared this at one of our seminars:

I married my husband when his daughter was seven and loved her as if she were my own. Over the years, her mother's bad-mouthing has totally turned her against me. Now I hate them both. I hope her mother's happy.

Of all the problems we hear about from all of our sources, be it Web site, consultations, support groups, or seminars, bad-mouthing stands alone as the single most common complaint. And it doesn't matter which stepwife is bad-mouthing. The point is that it is *never* okay.

When the husband remarries before his ex-wife, the ex-wife will feel she is in a two-against-one situation. She knows that her stepwife has heard not only her ex-husband's version of why the failed marriage was her fault but the version told by his friends and family as well. This automatically puts her on the defensive, making her feel more isolated and maligned than ever before.

Although mothers are by no means the only ones guilty of bad-mouthing, when they do so, their children will suffer its effects in a variety of ways. One scenario we hear over and over is when the mother bad-mouths the stepmother to the children, poisoning their minds against her whenever the opportunity arises. And even if the mother never experiences the repercussions of her own behavior, you can be certain her children will take the heat for her lack of self-control. The saddest part of all is that when their stepmom gets fed up with the way the children are treating her, she may eventually turn against them, often even refusing to talk to them when they're at her house. Is this what you really want for your children?

When the stepmother bad-mouths the ex-wife, it is just as ugly. If you are a stepmother, you need to be aware that children connect their identities with their parents, and any derogatory remark about their parents will quickly reflect back on them. When they are told, or overhear, that you think their mother is crazy or that all she cares about is money, it doesn't take them long to go from, "Your mother is crazy" to "Your mother is bad" to "I am bad." The resentment this engenders is detrimental, and they may never recover from the plummeting self-esteem you are setting into motion. If you don't want to be viewed as a wicked stepmother, it is imperative that you keep bad-mouthing in check.

The next time either of you feels yourself ready to open fire, consider the following options for developing the self-control necessary to resist the urge.

Stepwives:

- ❧ *Empathize and acknowledge feelings.* Think how bad it feels when someone bad-mouths your parents. Of course, *you* can complain about them all you want, but when you hear someone else do it, it is like a knife in the heart. And if it feels so bad to you as an adult, think about how it must feel to a child whose identity is even more tied into his parents.

- Start a private journal where you can acknowledge your innermost feelings about your stepwife and your situation. You may already be able to identify the overriding sensation of anger you feel. Determining what lies beneath the surface of that anger—feeling replaced or betrayed, for example—will help diffuse it before you bad-mouth.

- The next time you feel yourself ready to bad-mouth your stepwife for stepping on your toes, hold off long enough to distract yourself by listening to music, watching a movie, or taking a walk. Once you involve yourself in another activity, your anger will be diverted, as will the need to bad-mouth.

- Grin and bear it, take a deep breath, and count to ten. Let the breathing calm you physiologically while the counting occupies your mind. This has been proven to reduce the impulse to lose control, which can lead to bad-mouthing.

- Bite your tongue—literally. One of our clients swears she bit her tongue so much she actually developed calluses.

It doesn't matter which technique you choose to help yourself refrain from bad-mouthing. Just pick one and use it, use it, use it.

If It's Saturday, This Must Be Dad's House

When divorce occurs, instability reigns supreme as parents become preoccupied with trying to figure out how their new lives are going to work. When a stepmother enters the picture and the status quo is no longer adequate, everything gets shaken up one more time. And who's paying attention to the kids and their need for structure and consistency when all this jockeying is going on? All too often, the answer is *no one.*

After divorce, children may end up living in a home whose routines and rules are a little shaky. The problems double when they are required to live in two houses with two completely different sets of rules. And many times there is little to no communication between the homes or the adults who live in them. The children end up feeling like something between a pawn and a tennis ball, as they struggle to figure out what is expected of them. Here's how stepwives can help:

- Begin setting up a plan to *organize consistently* by focusing on specific areas such as discipline, following through on promises, being on time picking up or seeing your child, or setting up specific house rules or chores. Be aware of your own patterns of consistency, and commit to improving those areas in which you are inconsistent.

- Use the CoMamas What's Happening Form (at the back of the book) to communicate effectively with the other household.

What Kind of Child Is Yours?

Counseling children and families for over twenty-five years has given Dr. Krausz the expertise to help us develop the following profiles. Although there are many books that identify how children may feel after a divorce and remarriage, it is our goal to help stepwives learn how these children affect and are affected by the stepwife relationship.

Your (step)child will probably fit into one or more of the following profiles:

- The Lean on Me

- The I'll Make You Pay

- The Heartbroken

- The Scapegoat

- The Daydreamer

- The Don't Leave Me

The Lean on Me

> *As a little girl, Kathy was energetic, happy-go-lucky, and a great student. The older she got, the busier she became and the more she did for others. Only when she left to be on her own did her parents and stepparents see the problems. She was in one relationship after another that always ended with her mate feeling suffocated. Over the years, Kathy became more and more depressed because she couldn't seem to sustain a relationship.*

The Lean on Me seems able to handle everything for everybody, and it really looks as if this kid has it all together. He is a straight A student and teacher's pet, is emotionally tough, and appears very independent. But the resentment he feels over shouldering these burdens may not appear for years to come.

The Lean on Me may grow up to become what is commonly referred to as a caregiver or, in psychological jargon, codependent. This role may color their entire adulthood, from career choices all the way to their choice of mate. The Lean on Me becomes dependent on caring for others, trying to fix people and situations, and will face a lifetime of struggling with identity issues surrounding personal wants and needs. How can stepwives keep childhood intact for the Lean on Me, who seems to want to help out at every turn?

- *Empathize and acknowledge* his feelings of wanting to help out. Let him know that while you appreciate his efforts, this is his time to be a child. Lighten his load by taking back some of the responsibilities he has assumed. What you want to teach him is that is okay to have compassion for others without losing his sense of self.

- Help him focus on what is important to him rather than the family. If he seems to be taking on too much, encourage him to rest and engage in activities that interest him.

The I'll Make You Pay

Gloria called us after her child was expelled from school for the third time. By the time, she came in to see us, he had brought home another failing test grade. When she questioned him about it, he ripped it up and threw it in her face.

The I'll Make You Pay doesn't waste any time expressing his resentment. This child, beyond anger, is giving a very strong message: "You changed my life, and I'm going to make you pay!" He's into revenge and wants everyone to know who's to blame: his parents for the divorce and step-parents for barging into his life. They have all let him down, and he is prepared to do whatever he can to get back at them and make them suffer, just as he is.

When faced with children like this, many parents have a tendency to want to back off and loosen the reins, or go to the other extreme and become militaristic—exactly what you shouldn't do. Here is what you *should* do:

- Work closely with the school counselor, coach, care-takers, relatives, or any other significant person in the child's life to ensure consistency in all of his environments.

- You can teach your children that their parents are part of the solution rather than the problem by acknowledging their anger and other feelings regarding the divorce and remarriage. Empower them by positive modeling, and let them know you are not accepting their behavior, just their right to have their own feelings. This will help them feel less like victims.

- Observe the child closely, and try to be objective in your assessment of him. You need to be able to shape new behaviors. Rather than criticizing what he doesn't do, compliment him and his good behaviors. This will help him realize that positive attention is more rewarding than negative attention.

The Heartbroken

After his parents' divorce, Jeremy became sullen and withdrawn, often hiding out in his room. When his mother overheard him crying to his stuffed animals one day about how much he missed his dad, she knew she had to get some help.

Sad, lonely, and depressed, the Heartbroken is literally dying inside and may or may not be able to tell anyone just how badly he's feeling. But the signs are difficult to ignore if you know what you're looking for.

This child is often a loner who appears withdrawn much of the time, spending long periods in his room or some other isolated place. Don't confuse his silence and isolation with confidence and independence. In adolescence, watch him closely because he is in danger of entertaining suicidal thoughts or resorting to drug or alcohol abuse as a solution to his unhappiness. The Heartbroken needs your help right away:

- Come up with several activities you feel might be of interest to him. Even if he says, "I don't feel like it," set a date and participate in those activities with him. Starting with something low key will be less threatening. Stay involved until the warning signs disappear.

- Invite him to accompany you on simple, routine outings, such as grocery shopping or errands. Encouraging him to get out of his room and become more active will discourage him from wallowing in his feelings of hopelessness and helplessness.

⊷ If his withdrawn behavior or apathetic mood continues over several weeks, seek professional help.

The Scapegoat

*Claire's voice took on a sharp edge as she told us
how much her son reminded her of her ex. When we
brought this to her attention, she began to realize she had
been taking her anger toward her ex out on her son. This
was the beginning of her insight into how her feelings
about her ex were contributing to her son's behavior
problems.*

Heaven help the child who reminds a parent of the ex he
or she hates and is treated badly by that parent because of it.
It really doesn't matter what this child does; he will be dealt
with in words, gestures, and actions that convince him he is
not okay. Children treated this way in general may become
angry or turn their anger inward and become withdrawn
and depressed. Younger children can react by picking on
others, and older children may replace their family with
other kids who also feel they've been treated unjustly. The
collective anger from these children who are mad at the
world and want revenge creates a very frightening, volatile
situation. Here are some ideas about how to respond:

⊷ Keep your anger in check, and remember that the
child should *not* be held responsible for your feelings
toward your ex. Stay connected to the child, no matter
what age he is. He needs to know that you acknowledge his feelings and that he has importance in your
life, no matter what.

🐟 Help redirect the child's angry energy into something more positive, such as martial arts, boxing, or wrestling.

The Daydreamer

Since her parents' divorce and remarriage, five-year-old Cassandra seemed to live in a fantasy world. No matter who she spoke to, she referred to her mom, dad, sister, and brother as one big happy family, all living happily together in the same house. A concerned teacher alerted Cassandra's parents to the fact that her fantasy life was starting to affect her school and social activities, and they sought professional help for her.

The Daydreamer finds her fantasy world to be a much safer place than reality—a place where she really doesn't want to be. She seems to be in her own little world, and getting her attention is nearly impossible. Her innocent nature disguises the fact that she is unfocused, inattentive, and daydreaming much of the time. You can help her if you:

🐟 Encourage artistic outlets such as dance, writing short stories, drama, or music to help the Daydreamer outwardly express fantasy feelings.

🐟 *Talk and communicate effectively* with the child by making sure you have eye contact. Placing your hand softly on his shoulder will also help to get his attention. Repeating yourself over and over again in a louder tone will only cause this child to retreat emotionally.

The Don't Leave Me

Monique found it incredibly difficult to drop Saman-tha off at school each day because Sam would throw a tantrum, wrap herself around Monique's legs, and beg her not to leave. She felt so guilty leaving Sam and won-dered if her divorce and remarriage had anything to do with this behavior.

The Don't Leave Me wants to be with you all the time, and it seems she is always by your side. Her world was turned up-side down, and she feels anxious and afraid that other as-pects of her life will fall apart or someone will abandon her. Not having her parents in sight conjures up thoughts of more change, more fear. Statements such as "I can't," "This is too hard," or "Do this for me" reflect her insecurity or neediness. Maybe she's even a little manipulative. Telling her that school is fun or that visiting with her other parents will be great just will not fly with her. Instead:

❧ Gently yet firmly encourage her to do simple tasks, such as tying her shoes, sitting with a book by herself, or visiting a friend. Acknowledge her efforts with en-couraging words: "Great job" or "Thanks for doing that."

❧ Making her room at both houses a place she likes to sleep in will encourage her to become self-sufficient. Allowing her to sleep with a parent at one house when this same behavior is discouraged at the other creates confusion and an inconsistency that will sabotage in-dependence.

How Are You Treating the Children?

Answer the following questions to see if you are treating the children like POWs or respected dignitaries: Circle the answer that best fits your reply:

1. Do you put the kids first by:
   a. buying them every new fad that comes on the market?
   b. not speaking to them until they speak to you first?
   c. separating adult issues from child issues?
2. When you are angry with your stepwife, you:
   a. tell her she's crazy.
   b. tell the children she's crazy.
   c. gain self-control and write your feelings in your journal.
3. As the ex-wife and mother, you:
   a. tell your kids how much it would hurt you if they loved their stepmother.
   b. tell them they are traitors because they like their stepmother.
   c. tell them it's okay to form their own feelings about their stepmother.
4. The kids are acting out, so you:
   a. punish them by taking away TV.
   b. embarrass them by telling their friends what's been happening at home.
   c. try to discover what their feelings are.
5. The kids are disrespecting you as their stepmother, so you:
   a. stop speaking to them.
   b. tell their father to handle it.

   c. talk to them about the role you, as stepmother, want to play in their lives.

6. Your child is always ready to take care of everyone and everything, so you:
   a. give her more responsibility.
   b. tell her she has a problem and go get some help.
   c. let her know it's important for her to allow herself to be nurtured.

7. You've been called into school because your child has been disrupting the class, so you:
   a. excuse him from having to do anything.
   b. have a police officer talk to him.
   c. organize consistently with reasonable rules and expectations.

8. Your child lies around in his room all day, so you:
   a. buy him a new bed.
   b. don't allow him to come to the dinner table.
   c. find something he's interested in and become involved in it too.

9. There hasn't been much consistency since the divorce, so you:
   a. decide that you will have whatever rules you want in your own house.
   b. say dinnertime will be at 6:00 and never follow through.
   c. select some routines to share at both houses and stick to them.

10. Your stepdaughter reminds you of your husband's ex, so you:
   a. dye her hair purple.
   b. pick on her all the time.
   c. treat her like your own child because it's not her fault she looks like your stepwife.

If you answered *a* or *b* to every question, you need to consider how much of the child's behavior is coming directly from your attitude and behavior. If you answered *c* to every question, you are *putting the kids first,* and by doing so, treating them as respected dignitaries. Congratulations are in order.

Commonly Asked Questions

For children, divorce and remarriage represent a change in the close parent-child relationship they have always known. And although living in two households can provide additional role models and a wider variety of experiences, most kids are not thrilled about moving back and forth. Add volatile adult feelings to the mix, and it's easy to see why these children barely have a chance to lead healthy, happy lives. Following are some questions we are asked regularly regarding the children:

How can we handle sibling rivalry between all the kids in the extended-blended family? In any family, everyone needs a little space to be an individual, and this becomes even more important in the extended-blended family. Why would any child like having someone else's children in their life, playing with their toys, competing for the attention of their parents, or occupying space in their house? Create enough time and space for everyone to have some privacy. Even if they all have to share the same room, color-coding their toys or using tape to mark off some territory of their own will go a long way toward solving these problems.

My kids say they hate their stepmother. What can I do? When the children don't want to go to the other house or tell you they don't like their stepmother, it's time to apply the PRESCRPTON. Talk to them about why they are feeling this way, keeping in mind that children often try to elicit sympathy from the parent they're with by exaggerating what is going on at the other house. It's time for stepwives to present a united front. Talk to each other, claiming your part in how the children are feeling. If you are satisfied that the children's complaints are unfounded, you need to encourage them to maintain the schedule at both houses and even to call the other house when they're with you. This will prevent breaks in their feelings of attachment. If their complaints seem valid, review the advice in Chapter 8 and refer to Chapter 11.

What should I do when my kids don't want to go to the other house? So often human nature gets in the way of *putting the kids first.* We've been hurt by exes and stepwives and are secretly happy when the kids don't like them or want to be with them. Remembering that children who have both their mothers and their fathers in their lives have fewer difficulties in adulthood will help you go against your natural inclination to want to keep the kids with you and not with the ex.

Statistics overwhelmingly show that children who live with divorce have more suicides, commit more crimes, have more difficulties with relationships and marriage, and have higher incidences of drug, alcohol, and child abuse. But is divorce really what is at the root of all these problems? Might it not be instead the way adults in divorce situations handle their own passionate and confusing feelings? The degree to which children are affected is within the control of all the adults in the extended-blended family in which they live. That is why if you come away with only one thing from this entire book, you cannot afford to let it be anything other than *put the kids first.* And if you do that and nothing more, everything else will fall into place.

Chapter 10

How to Be in the Same Place at the Same Time ... and When "In-Laws" Behave Like "Out-Laws"

From inside the ex-wife's shoes, by Lynne:

> *For the entire fifteen years of my marriage, I loved the holiday season. It was a time to get together with friends and family and celebrate the abundance of life. Each year, I would hear what a sad time the holidays were for some people, and I just couldn't understand why. After my divorce, I felt the pain firsthand; now, the holidays represented painful reminders of the life I once had and the people I once loved.*

From inside the stepmother's shoes, by Louise:

> *Having been single much of my adult life, I had celebrated many a holiday with friends who hosted "orphans." It was always fun, but something was definitely missing. After I married Greg, the holidays took on a whole new meaning, and I looked forward to those special times, because now I had a child to spend them with. Greg and Evan had truly made my life better.*

Holidays, graduations, weddings, births, and all the rest are not about the events but about the relationships, and not just the stepwife relationship. Holidays and events may involve a whole cast of characters, including "in-laws" who often behave like "out-laws." All of you will need to learn how to put your feelings aside and get into the spirit of the occasion, whatever it is, if for no other reason but the kids. The best gift you can bestow on your children is to model for them the act of giving respect and cooperation to all the adults in their lives. Beginning with the winter holidays, this chapter will show you how it can be done.

The winter holidays are generally considered special because they aren't just one day but a whole season. Starting with Halloween and continuing on through New Year's, this period of time can be wonderfully festive and fun, or painful and depressing. Stepwives and their families generally find them painful and depressing. If you give in to the notion of the holiday blues, you may be setting yourself up for just that.

Halloween

One thing we have in common is our love of the holidays, especially Halloween. And in true stepwife fashion, Halloween was just one of the holidays we managed to ruin for each other.

Louise:

> *Lynne had pretty much decreed that I couldn't have any involvement in Evan's school events. Oh, I could help with homework, make his meals, and clean up after him, but my participation in any significant way was not allowed, and I was sick to death of it. My friends felt like I'd*

gotten a bum rap and tried to create activities I could be part of—outside of school—especially around the holidays.

It started out as such a casual thing really—a little haunted house for the kids in someone's living room. It was so much fun that the following year, we decided to do it again. That year, it got bigger and better, and we moved it to someone's garage. By the time Halloween 1992 rolled around, our haunted house had become almost legendary. People were begging to come see it, so one of the mothers got the idea to turn our private little weekend event into a fund raiser.

It was only later that I found out everyone in Evan's class got an invitation to the haunted house except Lynne, who then insisted I not even drive kids to the haunted house. Not only did she want to control me, she wanted to keep every last kid in the entire third-grade class from having anything to do with me! Needless to say, Halloween was ruined, and that wasn't even the end of it.

My heart stopped when I looked up from my desk in Greg's office the morning after to find Lynne standing in the doorway. The smell of her perfume lingered long after she sailed right past me, directly into Greg's office, making me feel once again that I had no right to be in my own life.

Lynne:

Louise had proved she would stop at nothing to push her way into Evan's life. She had a way of escalating *everything she was involved in, and when she was no longer satisfied participating in activities outside school, she began infiltrating his classroom events. "Who are you?" parents would ask when they saw me with Evan, followed by, "Oh, I thought Louise was Evan's mom." It seemed there was no way to make her understand that I was his mother and that chairing committees and being team mom were my rights, not hers. The Halloween party in 1992 was the breaking point. I had had enough.*

I arrived at school in full costume to help Evan's teacher with the class Halloween party, and just as the party was winding down, she asked if I'd be willing to take some kids to the haunted house she said Louise was hosting. It seemed the entire school had received an invitation—that is, everyone but me.

I was so angry I couldn't speak. I didn't know what to do. She had done it again—managed to exclude me from my own child's life—and I wasn't going to take it any more. Gone were my vows never to drag my family through the court system. I drove straight to an attorney's office and began filing a complaint against her. She had finally gone too far.

Everyone wants to participate in the Halloween festivities. The costumes. The haunted houses. Watching the kids' faces as they dump their bags of goodies on the floor the moment they walk in the door so they can revel in their stash. Here is how to go about it:

❧ Stepwives problem-solve by switching off every year. If the mother takes the kids trick-or-treating one year, their dad and stepmom take them the next. Or if there's a Halloween event at school, perhaps the mother can be the one to attend, and the father and stepmother can take the children trick-or-treating.

❧ *Organizing consistently* will go a long way in making this occasion run smoothly. If the kids are trick-or-treating with one set of parents, maybe they can get their costume with the other, and even get dressed for the big night at that house.

Kids look forward to Halloween months in advance. Don't ruin it for them by putting them in the middle of your issues with each other. In the big picture, there are very few years that children even want a parent to be part of their Halloween pleasure, so be mindful of working this out in advance.

Thanksgiving

Once stepwives learn to *talk and communicate effectively,* they may find out that their stepwife actually has some really good ideas or, in this case, recipes. After we became CoMamas, Lynne shared her traditional Thanksgiving recipes with Louise, and it turned out it was the best Thanksgiving meal Louise's family had ever eaten.

Stepwives:

❧ Agree to take turns here also, one year at Mom's, the next year at Dad's. If your children are going to the other house and you don't want to miss celebrating with them, create a mock Thanksgiving Day in advance of the real one. The event can still be very special. It's all what you make it.

Christmas or Hanukah

Shana wrote in and told us the following:

Things have gotten really bad for me. My ex and his wife won't even allow me to call their house, and I just found out that my kids were in a winter holiday pageant and I wasn't even invited!

Everyone should be entitled to participate in sharing in the holiday spirit with the kids. Holidays are about giving, and what better gift to give your children than to model that behavior yourself. No one should be excluded.

Sometimes you may need to celebrate Christmas or Hanukah in advance because the kids will be going out of town to be with your stepwife. If you want the Christmas holiday to feel authentic for them, you can address the question "How will Santa know where I'll be?" by letting them know that Santa makes concessions for children who have two families. He and his reindeer are available for deliveries in advance of December 24 but only in very, very special cases, like your child's.

Stepwives:

◄§ Apply the same switching strategy as for Thanksgiving. If you celebrate Christmas, have the children spend Christmas Eve at one house and Christmas Day at the other. And the next year, switch around. If Hanukah falls during the school year when the kids aren't on vacation, it can be celebrated during winter break so that everyone gets to enjoy the fun.

Mother's Day and Father's Day

> **We received the following e-mail:**
>
> I dread Mother's Day every year because I know I won't be acknowledged in any way. Why is it that step-mothers don't count at all on Mother's Day? We have joint custody of my stepson, I do everything for him, and yet I will never be considered good enough to celebrate Mother's Day. And my husband doesn't even get why I'm so upset over this.

We know this is "the" day reserved for a mom or dad, but it's a bit more complicated now, and you need to try and revise your way of thinking. Respect that your children have stepparents and that they deserve to be acknowledged too. Mothers and fathers need to share their day with their step-wife or Man on the Outside. Don't make the kids feel uncomfortable or disloyal if they want to do something nice for their stepparents. If sharing the day is out of the question, then it is your job to make sure you and your kids do something special for your spouse.

Parents' Birthdays

Of course, you should get to spend your birthday with your children, and we hope that all of you do. Because children need to learn the importance of acknowledging the people who love and care for them, it is up to you to make sure your children do just that. Take them shopping for a small gift, or have them make something at home for the parent whose birthday it is, so when the day comes, they have something to give or send. Once the stepmother or stepfather comes into the picture, it is appropriate for them to be responsible for the children's acknowledgment of their parents' birthdays and it's time for you to bow out.

Children's Birthdays

Two households celebrating the same child's birthday. Who throws the party? Where will it be, and who will get to go? Or will there be two parties? One suggestion we have is for one set of parents to host the birthday on the odd-numbered years and one set on the even years. Both sets of parents attend all the parties—assuming you are all comfortable being in the same room together. If you are not, one household should host the birthday party, and the other parents should celebrate separately. It's always a good idea to discuss the gift giving. Does a child really need two watches? Maybe both sets of parents can contribute for one combined gift.

School and Sporting Events

From the CoMamas' Web site:

My two kids spend most of their time with me. My ex just married a woman who has no children of her own. She and I have never even spoken, but all of a sudden she's been showing up at every school event, and I'm furious.

It's inevitable that your paths will cross at school and sporting events. When that time comes, be prepared to greet each other. A simple, "Hi, how are you?" will suffice. Do not ignore one another. It is rude and completely inappropriate.

And if you can do it, you might want to consider sitting together. It will make your children feel pretty great to look out in the audience and see all their parents together.

It is important that the husband let his ex-wife know in advance that her stepwife will be showing up. In the beginning, he may want to consider going alone, until his ex-wife can get used to the idea that there's another woman in her child's life—and in her life as well.

If you're still working on improving your stepwife relationship, you may want to devise a schedule so you don't have to spend every weekend together at these events. If the children play a sport, alternate weekends. Plan on everyone attending the awards ceremony, however, because this is something children are usually very proud of and they may want all their parents there.

Home Alone

Someone's going to be alone for the holidays, and if that someone is you, do *not* let your children know how badly you feel. They have their own feelings of loss and abandonment to contend with. No matter how tough it is for you, remember that you are the adult and it is up to you to put on a happy face, because they will take their cues from you. Let them know that although you will miss them, you will be okay, and what you want more than anything else is for them to have a good time.

Since your kids are going away, plan to spend the holidays with someone else you care about. Put things in perspective by making it a point to give to those less fortunate. Volunteer at a toy drive or soup kitchen, or adopt a family. When it's your turn to have the children for the holidays, keep in mind that the other parents aren't so lucky this year. Let them know that you understand they will miss the children.

Ex-wives:

&s If you are packing your children's bags, put a little gift in their luggage along with a note telling them to have a good time. You may even want to include some extra spending money.

Special Attention

> *Joey couldn't wait to see his dad. As his plane started its descent, Joey's excitement grew. He began thinking of all the stuff he needed to tell his dad and all the cool things they'd do together. He spotted his dad immediately and ran toward him, stopping dead in his tracks when he saw his stepmom. "Hey, dad," he said, ignoring Mary altogether.*
>
> *"What's wrong with that child?" Mary asked us, "I bend over backward every time he comes to town, and he barely speaks to me."*

If the children will be traveling to another city or state for an extended period of time, like winter or summer breaks from school, there are special needs to be aware of. They include acknowledging not being with their step- or half-siblings or adjusting to siblings they don't often see. Here are some ways to help them make the transition:

&s Little kids may be apprehensive about going to see their dad or mom or stepparents in another state. If they are very young and going on a plane, be sure they have an escort. On a special calendar, mark off the days until they will leave so the apprehension turns to anticipation. Have the child call the other parent to discuss what the activities will be when they arrive, so they can begin to prepare for their trip.

❧ Stepmothers need to be especially sensitive to step-children who are infrequent visitors by allowing them some alone time to bond with their fathers. This doesn't mean you shouldn't plan activities where you all participate. Just be sure to balance these times out.

❧ Teens may refuse to go to another city or state be-cause they don't want to be away from their friends, and they want to exert their independence. Be sensi-tive to what they will be giving up. *Empathize and ac-knowledge* how difficult you know it is for them, but remind them how much the other parent loves them. Beginning these discussions early will help

❧ Make sure you have a special place for them when they come to your house. If you can do it, set up a room that is just theirs. If this isn't possible, provide some-thing designated just for them: sleeping bag or sheets and blanket or a placemat with their name on it. Let them know that they aren't just visitors, but that your home is their home too.

❧ *Talk and communicate effectively* with the children about the family they may be missing but without grilling them. Children often feel like double agents, asked to infiltrate enemy lines by one parent or the other. Encourage them to talk about what they do when they're not with you, but *set limits and bound-aries,* letting them know you're interested but that you also respect the privacy of their other home.

When children behave badly during the holidays, calmly *set limits and boundaries,* and don't require their full participation or emotional involvement. They may be acting out because they are feeling disloyal to their other parent by being with you. Remind them, without making them feel guilty, that their other parent is missing them. Help or encourage them to call or write. They may feel uncomfortable doing this, so let them know that it is fine to want to communicate with the parent they're not with. Be sure to spend some extra time with them while they're in town. Take time off work or use your vacation days.

Pomp and Circumstance

> *Jaime was her college class valedictorian, and her entire family was bursting with pride. Not only that, but everyone was planning on attending the ceremony. Jaime was so preoccupied with how they would all get along that she stumbled through her well-rehearsed speech.*

Graduations are one-time events. Remember that they cannot be replayed if they don't go well. As we write this book, Evan is getting ready for his long-awaited high school graduation, and like most other seniors, he is more than ready to go, and go he will. It's hard for us to even say these words without getting all choked up. But at least we know that these major milestones in his life will be celebrated with anticipation and joy by all of us. The usual trepidation and dread that for over a decade surrounded every event in his life will not be a part of this day. We can't say it enough: the absolute best part of being CoMamas is what it has done for Evan.

Whether you are CoMamas or not, sometimes outside circumstances dictate the course of events. You can handle them with dignity and respect by using the advice below:

- ❧ If there are only two tickets available, the mother and the father are entitled to the tickets, even if one of them participates in the child's life only on a limited basis—unless there is a court order prohibiting such contact.

- ❧ If there are more than two tickets, as a general rule they should go to the siblings first. If there are enough tickets for all the children, the stepparents should determine which one will—go by drawing straws, or through some other random method.

Here Comes the Bride and the Blessed Event

Mycala couldn't wait to plan her wedding. When she told her mother, Mona, that her stepmom would also be seated at the head table, Mona blurted out, "Why is she allowed to rob me of every happy event in your life?" Mycala couldn't believe her mother would ruin her special day with this stuff. Brokenhearted, she eloped to avoid all of them.

Weddings for people with divorced parents can be a nightmare. By the time children from divorced families are ready to marry, they may have distanced themselves from parents and stepparents still at war, or perhaps they have just learned to accept their situation. Either way, they have a host of decisions to make, and it's up to you to make sure you don't add to their burden. If you do, they might just run off to a justice of the peace and avoid the whole thing. Here are some important things to remember when planning the wedding:

◆ If you are hosting a daughter's wedding, at the very least make sure her stepparent's families are included on the guest list. If you can, enlist your stepwife's help in planning the event. Any gesture you are comfortable with will be greatly appreciated by your stepwife.

◆ *Remember realistic expectations* regarding your role during the planning and the wedding. Your children will have their future spouse's family to take into consideration now as well as their own extended-blended family. And if that person comes from a divorced family, the complications will increase exponentially.

◆ Understand what your children expect from each of you. If they want their mother and father to walk them down the aisle, respect their wishes. Let them know that it is okay to want this, and as uncomfortable as it might be for you, do it. It is, after all, their day.

◆ If you are the stepparent who is sitting out while the bride or groom's parents fully participate, you must remember not to take this as a personal slight. *This isn't about you.* This is just one more opportunity for you to *put the kids first.*

You would think that by this point, everything should have worked itself out and stepwives should be getting along. But if you haven't worked out your issues or you've only recently become stepwives, your problems will not be resolved in time for the blessed event—the birth of your grandchildren. If you've carried your battle this far, you need to know that it has got to stop, and it is never too late to make the necessary changes for everyone to get along. Not everyone has to go to every event. If you miss a school play or a baseball game, it's not the end of the world. But if you aren't able to attend the birth of your grandchildren, it would be very unfortunate. Let your children know how delighted you are at the impending birth of your grandchild. Share with them that you will do everything in your power to create an atmosphere where everyone will be comfortable, because if your presence creates animosity, they may just ask you not to come at all, and they would be well within their rights.

What Makes In-Laws Out-Laws?

"Calm down, honey," John said to his wife, Yvette, as they discussed his mother's wedding plans. "I will not calm down," screeched Yvette. "The nerve of your mother, asking your ex-wife to be her matron of honor! There's no way I'm going to that wedding, and if you really love me, you won't go either."

Every event feels like torture for stepwives when in-laws behave like out-laws. One of the many lines that often get blurred in the stepwife relationship is that of the family. The ex-wife wonders how she can go from being an integral part of someone's family, sharing holidays, special occasions, and every event in between, and then—nothing. Suddenly she's been cut off from people she's known and loved as if she'd never even existed. And the current wife feels that this is *her* family now. Is there anyplace the ghost of the ex-wife doesn't linger?

There weren't many things we agreed on over the years. In fact, there was hardly anything we did agree on, except our feelings for our mother-in-law: we both loved Meribeth. And although we were lucky because Meribeth was never an out-law, that didn't mean we didn't resent each other's relation-ship with her.

In-laws often feel caught in the middle and aren't sure where their loyalty should lie. They are forever connected to the mother of their grandchildren and may have even been there to support her during the births. They never consid-ered the possibility that their grandchildren's parents would no longer be together, let alone that they would have a new daughter-in-law to get used to. And even if they know what the protocol is, what do they do with their feelings? How do they pick sides?

In-laws need to make the decision of whether to shun their ex-daughter-in-law or stand by her side. And each choice has ramifications: upset their son and his wife, or upset the mother of their grandchildren. Their son will probably be angry with them if they stay too connected to his ex-wife and don't embrace his new wife. In-laws need to remember that as much as they might have loved their ex-daughter-in-law, even considered her a daughter, she is not their child, and their main loyalty should be to their son and his wife. Unless the situation is handled carefully, how-ever, the ex-wife is certain to be devastated by the rejection of her former in-laws. But if their son asks that they not in-vite his ex-wife to family gatherings where he and his new wife will be, they need to respect that request. Stepmothers have the right to enjoy family functions without *her* being there.

Ex-wives:

- ❧ If you feel connected and want to continue a relationship with your ex-husband's family, do so separately. Arrange to see them or speak with them at a time when he and your stepwife are not going to be there. In other words, don't expect to be invited for Thanksgiving, but do have lunch with them.

- ❧ Accept the fact that your stepwife is part of his family now. Don't resent her for this. She is entitled to participate in family functions and develop her own relationship with them, just as you did.

In-laws can't ignore the fact that their ex-daughter-in-law still exists. When they see their son with his wife and children, they need to ask about the mother, even if this offends the stepmother. This will make the children feel that their mother is still important. What the stepmother must accept is that her stepwife was part of this family and that her children are still. However, in-laws must make a special effort to make the stepmother feel welcome, because if the stepmother feels that her new in-laws are favoring her stepwife, she may try to pull her husband away from his family to balance the scales. This could ultimately damage the relationship they have with their son and grandchildren and affect their time with them.

Stepmothers:

- ❧ *Empathize with and acknowledge* your stepwife's feelings. This was her family first, and losing them is just one more loss in a long list she must endure because of her divorce.

◆§ Don't bad-mouth your stepwife to your new family or participate in any discussions about her. It will only make you look small. If they want a relationship with her, respect that fact. It should in no way diminish the relationship you have or can have with them.

◆§ Encourage your family to get to know or have a relationship with your stepchildren. Children usually love big families, and they will appreciate or grow to appreciate your family.

Commonly Asked Questions

Good or bad, big events are here to stay, and they usually involve families' coming together . . . or apart. How can you make the best of these situations when you're all at odds with each other? The following questions have come up over and over again:

Should we all spend holidays together? Spending the holidays together is a personal choice. In most cases, there is so much animosity between everyone that this is an impossibility. Under normal circumstances, we suggest setting *limits and boundaries* on who attends each event. However, weddings, graduations, and births are the big events that occur so infrequently they call for extraordinary measures. These events require that everyone attend, so you may want to dig down deep, muster up your courage, and all celebrate together. The biological parents should always be the primary players at these big events. However, the stepparents should not be overlooked. There is a difference between taking a back seat and riding in the trunk.

How can I teach my kids values when they get so much from so many people? Gift giving and receiving can be a good news-bad news kind of thing when it comes to the extended-blended family. Often in-laws and out-laws want to acknowledge the new children and make them feel welcome. The easiest way to do this is to give gifts, and sometimes they tend to overdo it. To help the kids make sense of all this, discourage the onslaught of gifts. We suggest assigning each child to a family member, which will keep gift giving to a minimum and teach the children to appreciate what they have. Make sure you curtail your own shopping frenzy, as it's easy for stepwives to try and outdo each other. It's crucial for everyone to remember that the way to your child's heart should not be through your pocketbook.

Should an ex attend the funeral of former in-laws? We consulted with a stepwife, who shared the following: "My father passed away recently, and my ex and his wife insisted I not take my kids to the funeral. *They* didn't think it was appropriate." Not all the big events are happy ones, and the circle of life unfortunately ends with death. And as most of us know, death is very painful to those left behind, especially if you have unfinished business with that person. When you're divorced from someone, you're also divorced from their family, but does that mean you shouldn't show respect and convey your condolences to the family you were once a part of and your children are still connected to? Whether you do it in person, by phone, or with a note will depend on the relationship you have with them at the time. If you choose to attend the funeral or service, discuss it with your ex. Will it make him or her uncomfortable if you're there? If you bring your new spouse? If the answer is yes, be considerate of those wishes.

. . .

When it comes to raising children, the days are long and the years pass by too quickly. Remaining cognizant of how your behavior affects your children every single day of their lives will help diminish the growing pains in the stepwife relationship. Do it now so you won't have to spend the rest of your life trying to undo the damage you may have caused along the way.

Situations That Go Beyond the Normal

> Tracy was ordered by the courts to go into an alcohol treatment program before she could have unsupervised visits with her daughter, Rachel. Arriving intoxicated at her ex's home, she demanded to see her daughter. An argument ensued, and Tracy and her ex began a tug of war, each pulling on one of Rachel's arms. Intervening, her stepmom grabbed Rachel and ordered Tracy off her property, threatening to call the police. Crying and feeling ashamed of her actions, Tracy left, vowing she would never take another drink.

Most of the situations in this book are commonplace and workable, but some circumstances require intervention by a specialist. This chapter will address the most common addictions and mental health problems Dr. Krausz has seen in her practice that affect stepwives and their families. If you recognize one of the problems in this chapter, we suggest you get information about the problem, get help from the appropriate specialist, and make the necessary changes.

A specialist will help you become more objective in relating to a stepwife or ex who has an addiction or mental health problem. It is difficult for anyone to think clearly when entrenched in an emotional and confusing relationship. Having accurate information that comes from a professional will help you make the best possible decisions for you and your family. While we've listed some of the behaviors associated with addiction and mental health problems for you to use as assessments, they are not to be used as complete diagnostic tools. They can help determine the degree of severity and whether your situation warrants professional intervention.

Alcoholism

With one in every thirteen adults, and nearly 14 million Americans overall abusing alcohol, it's not surprising that 53 percent of men and women have stated that one or more of their close relatives have a drinking problem. Besides the physical consequences of alcohol such as cirrhosis of the liver, brain damage, or harm to the fetus during pregnancy, drinking can emotionally affect children, families, careers, and relationships.[1]

The following behaviors can help you to evaluate whether you, your stepwife, Man in the Middle, or Man on the Outside have alcoholic tendencies:

- A strong need or compulsion to drink

- The inability to stop drinking after starting

- Withdrawal symptoms when alcohol use is stopped

- The amount of alcohol needed to feel a buzz has increased

- Failure with tasks at work, school, or home

- Drinking while driving or operating machinery

❧ Continuing legal problems as a result of drinking (e.g., arrest for driving under the influence or for physical abuse)

❧ Relationships that suffer as a result of continued drinking[2]

Don't Be Fooled

Perhaps you've said to yourself, or heard your ex or stepwife say, "I've changed my drinking habits. I don't drink the hard stuff any more. I've switched to beer and wine!" Many alcoholics tend to think that if they change the type of liquor they're drinking, they really don't have an alcohol problem. This is a myth. According to both the National Institute on Alcohol Abuse and Alcoholism and Alcoholics Anonymous, it doesn't matter what type of alcohol one drinks, how long one has been drinking, or specifically how much alcohol one consumes.[3] The important factor is the craving an individual has for alcohol. This craving is as strong as the need for food and water, and makes it very difficult for many individuals to stop drinking on their own. Current research suggests that although many people have a genetic vulnerability to alcoholism, environmental influences are as important as, if not more important than, genetic ones.[4]

No matter who has the drinking problem, relationships between stepwives, the exes, and children will be affected. Alcoholism in any form has an effect on communication and *problem-solving.* It will be difficult to *organize consistently* because the alcoholic is in turmoil and can't even get her own life together, let alone co-parent with her stepwife.

The Children Are at Risk

Casey and his younger brother, Jimmy, saw their dad, Larry, and stepmom on weekends. The adults remained drunk most of the time, leaving Casey to become the "alcohol detective" and protector of Jimmy. Finally, Casey refused to go with Jimmy to his dad's. After a night of drinking, Larry woke up one morning to realize that Jimmy had taken off. He panicked and called his ex and eventually the police. To everyone's relief, Jimmy returned after dark. While Larry screamed at Jimmy, blaming him for leaving the house, his stepmom sat silently by, hung over. Jimmy's mom vowed to take Larry back to court for full custody, and Casey felt guilty for not being there to protect his brother.

The affects of alcoholism on children's lives can be severe. It is common knowledge that children of alcoholics are at greater risk for having psychiatric problems compared with children whose parents are not alcoholics. They are four times as likely to become alcoholics themselves. With these numbers, it is not surprising that one in five adult Americans has been brought up with an alcoholic parent.[5]

Take the time to observe the children. Are they:

- Depressed or angry because they can't do anything about the situation?

- Worried a lot about the parent who is drinking?

- Concerned for the safety of the nonalcoholic parent?

If you answered yes to any of the above, be aware that these are common feelings children have as a result of living with an alcoholic parent. The communication in an alcoholic environment is filled with mixed messages creating confusion for the children. One minute they feel loved, the next neglected or abused. Their schedules constantly change. Worrying about whether they will be picked up, get dinner on time, or have any specific bedtime distracts them from being able to focus on "kid stuff." Often children think that they were the cause of the parent's drinking and feel guilty.

Early experience in an alcoholic environment affects children's feelings and perceptions about their world even after they leave home and become adults. Not being able to trust the most important parental role models early on in their lives creates enormous problems within the relationships of adult children of alcoholics. The cycle continues.[6]

Children often keep alcoholism a secret. Consider the questions below to assess whether the child is experiencing symptoms related to being in an alcoholic environment or is abusing alcohol himself:

- Depression. Does he seem to be withdrawn or have suicidal thoughts?

- Antisocial. Does the child have few friends or none at all?

- Psychosomatic complaints. Does he complain of frequent stomachaches, headaches, or fatigue?

- Aggression. Does he display violent or aggressive actions toward others?

❧ Steals or lies. Are you constantly questioning where the child is or if items are missing from your home?

❧ Truant. Are you continually called by the school because of attendance issues? Is the child failing?

❧ Drugs or alcohol. Is the child showing symptoms of drug or alcohol abuse?[7]

A yes answer to any of the above behaviors should be a red flag to parents and warrants professional help.

Some children of alcoholics become overly responsible and take on the parental role. They become driven, strive toward perfection, and can display great leadership qualities in school. These traits are to be commended, but because these children drive themselves so hard, they end up subject to tremendous internal pressure.

It seems to be easier for these children to control their school environment than the one at home. Unfortunately, the ill effects of being raised by an alcoholic parent will most likely catch up with them later in life. When these children become adults, they will try to fix everyone and their problems. Not feeling in complete control of their environment, their relationships, whether personal, social, or work related, will take a hard hit. With no intervention, addictive behaviors can be passed down from one generation to the next.

Many stepwives have asked us what they can do if the alcoholic is unwilling to seek help. Here are some suggestions:

❧ *Talk and communicate effectively* with the drinker right after an alcohol-related problem occurs, and let him know how you feel about his drinking. Acknowledge feelings the alcoholic may express.

- Discuss the consequences (not punishment) of his behavior if he does not get help. For example, he will see the children only under supervision because of safety issues; visitation will be limited; the children may be removed from the alcoholic environment.

- Be prepared to give information about different treatment options. Consult the Resources section of this book.

- Organize an intervention by getting help from a therapist, family members, or other friends to confront the drinker in a group.

Drug Abuse

At age forty, Jerry left his wife of twenty years and married a twenty-two-year-old woman. Using cocaine and other stimulants, Jerry and his new wife began abusing drugs together. He saw his children less and less, and his child support checks stopped coming. He was fired from his job and found himself sinking into a deep depression. A drug overdose landed him in the emergency room, then back at family court, where he was told to seek treatment for his drug addiction. Realizing the impact drugs had on him and his children, Jerry slowly began the uphill battle to turn his life around.

Drug abuse, like alcoholism, is an addiction. It affects not only the addict but those around him. Because the behavior of an addict can be quite erratic, many stepwives are afraid to say or do anything about it. But if you choose to do nothing, the consequences can be tremendous. Someone may be abused, injured, or die. Get the support you need, and keep the children and yourself safe.

The following behaviors can help you determine whether drug abuse may be present:

❧ Nausea, vomiting, shakiness

❧ Change in sleeping patterns (too much or too little)

❧ Constant sniffling from the nose, runny nose, cough

❧ Associating with a new group of friends, especially with those who use drugs

❧ Excessive talking

❧ Needle marks on body

❧ An abrupt change in mood and attitudes, agitation

❧ Sudden and continuing decline in attendance or performance at work or in school

❧ Impaired relationships with family members or friends [8]

If you have noticed any of these behaviors, medical as well as psychological help is necessary. Seek out a professional who can offer life-saving treatment and support.

Here is what you can do when interacting with someone with an addiction:

- *Keep the children safe.* Seek intervention to remove the children from the environment if need be.

- Learn to *set limits and boundaries* by clearly stating what behavior will not be tolerated (any addictions).

- *Talk and communicate effectively* about the consequences of any further addictive behavior (no visitation or supervised-only visitation).

- Stay strong. *Nurture yourself* by taking a class on stress management

- Staying strong doesn't mean you keep everything bottled up inside. The more you talk about your fears, concerns, and expectations, the more centered you will become, and it won't be quite so easy for you to get sucked into the whirlpool of addiction.

Emotional, Physical, and Sexual Abuse

His ex-wife continues to call and threaten me. I try to defend myself, but to no avail. My husband seems helpless and unsupportive. What am I doing here? These aren't my kids, and I'm getting sick of this. I'm doing the best I can. I don't want to leave my marriage, but nothing seems to work.

You know when you've been verbally abused. You hear name calling or bad-mouthing, you receive a barrage of hor-

rible words, or you hear that tone of voice. You are being dis-
respected. You can take it, or you can choose to give it right
back. But two stepwives yelling at each other will only escalate the situation. While verbal abuse is easy to recognize,
emotional abuse—being ignored, constantly talked to in a
sarcastic tone, incessantly teased, or put down in front of
others—is more subtle.

Abuse is not acceptable in any form. When your stepwife
is verbally or emotionally abusive, *set limits and boundaries* by using "I" statements: "When I hear you scream at
me, I don't feel comfortable continuing the discussion. I
want to be able to listen and understand what you are feeling. When you are ready to talk in a more respectful manner, I will be more than happy to speak with you."

If your stepwife, ex, or child continues to abuse you ver
bally, let them know you will talk to them later. You have the
right to remove yourself from an abusive situation, whether
you walk away or hang up the phone. Remember that you are
not ignoring or disrespecting the individual; you are ignoring the behavior. You can then make an attempt to talk to
the individual at another time.

> *My children's stepmother hits my kids with a belt. I've
> confronted her about it, and she screamed at me for inter-
> fering in her and my ex's lives. She said that's how she
> was brought up and that they'll raise the kids any way
> they want when they're with them. She thinks she's
> teaching my kids respect. My kids are afraid to go to their
> home. It's impossible to talk to my ex or stepwife. I'm
> going to call the police.*

In 1998, it was reported that approximately 903,000 children were victims of child abuse or neglect. That amounts

to a rate of 12.9 per 1,000 children younger than eighteen years of age being abused by parents or other relatives.[9] Abuse creates not only visual but emotional bruises. We have heard about stepwives attacking each other, and while they can go and receive support and safety if they so choose, children are more vulnerable. When they are hurt, they do not have the same capacity to go for help.

It is not uncommon for children who have been physically abused to display the behaviors listed below. Any of these behaviors that apply to your child or stepchild requires intervention immediately:

- Relationship problems

- School problems

- Drug or alcohol abuse

- Depression

- Anger or violence

- Low self-esteem

- Physical marks and bruises on their bodies

- Sexual abuse

Sexual abuse is reported in the tens of thousands in the United States, yet many incidents are not accounted for because of the stigma and shame associated with it. Sexual abuse can occur within families and stepfamilies and by friends, teachers, or strangers. To confront and process this ultimate betrayal is a must. The younger the victim is, the more confused he or she is between love, loyalty, and feeling that something is wrong. The child may have been threatened or told not to share the "special secret."

Proving a child has been molested is one of the more challenging tasks therapists, child protective services personnel, and family courts deal with. This is not an uncommon accusation made by exes during a divorce or when a stepmother comes into the picture. Because it is one adult's word against the other, the court often has a tough time sifting through the facts. To convict a parent or stepparent of molestation or disallow the child's visitation with them is difficult because it's not always clear that the accusation is real. If the child is able to verbalize his experiences to a parent, teacher, or trained therapist, there is a better chance of clarifying the situation. The dynamics below will help you evaluate the possibility of a child's experiencing sexual abuse:

- ❧ Promiscuity or sexual acting out

- ❧ Nightmares, sleep disturbances

- ❧ Negative statements about their bodies

- ❧ Fear of leaving home

- ❧ Delinquency

- ❧ Violent behavior

- ❧ Sexual themes in artwork[10]

While nightmares and sleep disturbances and the fear of leaving home may be related more to a phase in the child's development, when combined with the other symptoms, there is a greater indication that sexual abuse may be present. Don't second-guess these behaviors; your child's health and safety are at risk.

. In teaching children about the dangers of sexual abuse, parents and stepwives need to *talk and communicate effectively* with the children about not letting anyone touch their bodies in any way. Teach them to tell an adult if someone tries to touch their private parts or talks to them in a "bad way." If abuse has occurred, let the child know that it was not his fault. Take him to a physician to be checked. Remove the child from the dangerous environment, and seek counseling immediately.

Mental Health Problems

Most of us are not deranged individuals out to ruin someone's life or family, so why is it we often hear from stepwives, "My stepwife has a personality disorder"? Before you diagnose your stepwife as having any kind of personality disorder, it is imperative that you have an idea of what these disorders really entail.

Mental illness strikes one out of five adults, or an estimated 22.1 percent of Americans age eighteen and older.[11] The most common disorders are, depression, bipolar disorder (formerly known as manic-depressive disorder), schizophrenia, anxiety disorders, and obsessive-compulsive disorder.

Depression

After her husband left her, Ana became very depressed. She wasn't able to get out of bed in the morning to get her children off to school, and the children were burdened with many responsibilities. Comments by her stepwife and ex, calling her lazy and an unfit mother, only exacerbated her despondent feeling. Ana felt as though she were sinking into a hole so deep she would never come out.

While a major depressive disorder can manifest itself in behaviors such as Ana's, one can continue functioning at work and home but with great effort and distress. Chronic and mild forms of depression affect approximately 18.8 million American adults and nearly twice as many women as men.[12] Divorce and the stresses associated with co-parenting can cause depression in stepwives, Men in the Middle, and children.

Depression has been researched extensively, and the good news is that with counseling and medication, most depressed clients can feel better. The bad news is that if it is left untreated, suicide or homicide can be the result.

We now have the tools to better diagnose depression in children, so it is important to know about this illness, not just to understand your stepwife but because children are affected as well. Judith Wallerstein, Julia Lewis, and Sandra Blakeslee, in their latest book, *The Unexpected Legacy of Divorce,* found that children feel a greater sense of sadness, loneliness, and anger postdivorce or remarriage because of the many situations they are exposed to.[13] These situations include angry stepwives and exes, the adjustment of living in two homes, having to fly alone to see a parent, and the constantly changing schedules. The following behaviors will help you to determine if anyone in your extended-blended family is depressed:

- ❧ They are sad most of the day.

- ❧ They have lost or gained weight.

- ❧ They sleep too little or too much.

- ❧ They feel tired every day.

- ❧ They feel worthless.

- ❧ They are consumed with excessive guilt.

- ❧ They have recurrent thoughts of hurting themselves or fear death.

- ❧ Their symptoms affect their social and work situations.

- ❧ Medical reasons (thyroid, diabetes, bereavement) for the behavior have been ruled out.[14]

These behaviors do not appear overnight. They gradually take over your life and become unbearable. Between 80 and 90 percent of people with depression can be helped.[15] Check the Resources section in the back of the book for sources of support.

Bipolar Disorder

We know that many women have felt that their stepwife is not just depressed but also sometimes seems to have way too much energy. A bipolar diagnosis consists of mood swings that can involve a combination of mania and depression in various degrees and cycles. This particular mood disorder has a tendency to run in families. If you are concerned that a child is being exposed to extreme behaviors and is modeling them, or there is a concern genetically, seek professional help.

Schizophrenia

Schizophrenia is the most immobilizing and long-term illness of all the major mental illnesses. Many of the behaviors may be perceived as acceptable and somewhat eccentric, until they go too far, such as with a psychotic episode in which an individual has lost touch with reality. Schizophrenia is complex and still puzzling to researchers. The real disorder of schizophrenia affects approximately 1 percent of men and women equally within our population.[16] The symptoms described below apply to both men and women:

- Delusions

- Hallucinations

- Disorganized speech

- Disorganized behavior

- Social and occupational dysfunction

Individuals with schizophrenia view the world from their own perspective, as we all do, but their world is very different from the norm, for they often feel anxious, detached, and preoccupied. Their thoughts can be paranoid and filled with delusions of persecution or grandeur. Internal voices may tell them what to do, think, or say. Of course, not being able to sort out what is relevant and what is not is contrary to developing a stable relationship between stepwives.

> *After many years, Jack divorced Linda, who was diagnosed with schizophrenia, and married Carol. Living out of her car, Linda frequently showed up unannounced to visit her children and ask for money. Feeling sorry for her, Carol and Jack gave her money. However, the more they gave, the more she wanted. Talking to Linda rationally never seemed to make any difference, and when Linda accused Carol of conspiring to "control her mind," Carol became concerned and scared for herself and the children.*

For the sake of the children and the stepwife relationship, it would be best if the schizophrenic individual stayed in treatment, but this rarely happens. Whether medicated or not, your stepwife with schizophrenia will probably be in and out of your life. Statistically, this is not an illness to be feared. Acknowledge its existence by encouraging the individual to seek help through support groups, residential care, family therapy, and self-help groups.

Anxiety Disorders

> *Janice, age seventeen, came into counseling complaining about her stepmom. "She's always on my case to clean everything. I can't put a glass down without her running to pick it up. The pictures in my room have to be perfectly straight on the wall. She vacuums all the time. It drives me crazy. My mom calls her a neat freak, but that doesn't*

> *make me feel any better. My dad just says she just wants to have a clean house, and I need to be more responsible. I can never please her. I hate living with her."*

If you've never felt stress in your stepwife relationship, congratulate yourself because you would be one of a kind. We all experience stress. Whether it's a positive feeling you get from the child's graduation or the stress of being bad-mouthed by your stepwife, it is stress nonetheless.

Stress within the stepwife relationship can be so great that one can develop an anxiety disorder. Anxiety is a generalized fear that seems to come on for no apparent reason. More than 19 million people are affected by this very common problem which includes panic attacks, obsessive-compulsive disorder, posttraumatic stress disorder, generalized anxiety, and phobias.[17] It is important to have a thorough medical exam to rule out any medical cause for the anxiety such as high blood pressure, diabetes, or thyroid disease. Often stepwives with anxiety disorders self-medicate with alcohol and drugs.

Obsessive-Compulsive Disorder

This particular diagnosis involves recurring thoughts (obsessions) and behaviors (compulsions) that seem to have a life of their own. Attempting to stop these behaviors creates lots of anxiety. Anxiety in any form—social phobia or panic attacks—limits the interaction stepwives can have with each other and the significant people in their lives. It affects marriages, divorces, children, and quality of life. Once recognized, treatment is available through counseling and medication.

Most Commonly Asked Questions

Understanding the dynamics of abuse and mental health problems will give you a better idea of how to deal with situations that go beyond the normal. These most commonly asked questions stem from an individual's observation and concern about behaviors or moods that seem out of the ordinary for the person who is suspected to be on drugs.

I don't want to accuse my child of being on drugs if it's not true. What do I do? If you suspect your child is on drugs, express your concern to your ex or stepwife, and ask for their thoughts. Talk with your child regarding your concerns. If he won't talk with you, let him know that you love him too much to let this potential problem go unaddressed. You also have the right as a parent to search his room for drug paraphernalia, read his journal, and talk to his friends. Even if you don't find drugs but his mood is still contrary to his usual behavior, you need to remain vigilant and not allow yourself to develop a false sense of security. This could be a life-or-death matter. Seek professional help.

I found welts on my child's body when he came back from his dad's. Is this discipline? Any time you find marks on your child's body beyond the usual scrapes and bruises, it's time to investigate. It may be physical abuse and should never be tolerated. Talk to your ex about what you saw, and let him know that until he gets counseling and learns to control his anger, you must *put the kid first* and keep him or her with you. Institute further consequences and strategies (see the Resources section) to ensure the safety of the child.

Is it normal for my stepwife to ignore the kids and do nothing all day? Sometimes it's not only the child's behavior you need to keep an eye on, but your stepwife's as well. If you hear about a reduction in her activity level, it's possible your stepwife is depressed. Whether she is still grieving over the loss of her marriage, is overwhelmed by her living situation, or is genetically predisposed to depression, it is important to talk with her regarding your concerns. You should actively *empathize and acknowledge* her feelings, and let her know that you would like to assist her in getting some help. If she chooses not to speak with you, contact a friend or family member who can intervene. Depression is a quiet disease. By bringing it to the table and addressing this problem, you will be helping her and *putting the kids first.* They deserve to have a parent they know and love, and she has a right to feel in control of her life again.

CoMamas Commandments

Step into her shoes.

Use the PRESCRPTON daily as a preventive measure, not just when problems occur.

Admit you've both been wrong in the past, and focus on what you can do right in the future.

Give your stepwife the benefit of the doubt when she does something you don't like.

Work the program alone. You don't need your stepwife to work with you to be successful.

Expect backsliding.

The CoMamas can be reached at:

760-942-4572 (phone)
760-918-0680 (fax)
feelgood@comamas.com (e-mail)
www.comamas.com (Web site)

Epilogue

From the CoMamas Web site, Mother's Day 2001.
A tribute to my CoMama, by Louise:

Ten years have passed since Lynne and I officially became stepwives, and as you all know, it hasn't been an easy road for either of us. But we were fortunate after all these years finally to become CoMamas. And as I get to know Lynne, I've come to appreciate her generosity and beautiful spirit, but never more than in the last few weeks.

My Greg was suddenly and without warning stricken with a life-threatening illness, and in just a few short days I learned the meaning of complete and total fear. When Lynne heard about Greg, her only thought was how she could help me. I will never forget the genuine concern and love she showed as we cried together. She was there for me every single day, and without her strength and support, I don't know how I would have survived the long, lonely days sick with worry and dread.

Miraculously, Greg recovered, and when I look back through the years, I realize now there were many times Lynne put her own feelings aside and I was the beneficiary of that benevolence. And as Mother's Day approaches, a day that Lynne has shared with me all these years, I am grateful that she is my CoMama.

A tribute to my CoMama, by Lynne:

It was three years ago almost to the day that Louise and I stood in my driveway arguing over a pair of shoes.

Since that time, through our laughter and our tears, we have discovered we have a lot more in common than just a pair of strappy sandals and a man. The most important thing we have always shared is our love for my most precious treasure, my son, Evan.

Louise met Evan when he was only five years old and has loved him ever since. It wasn't easy for me to accept, and I spent years wishing he would hate her. Instead, he gave her what she deserved: his love and respect. I don't know how I can possibly even begin to thank her for the gift of love she has given him over the years or for the joy and stability she has brought to his life and for spending almost a third of her life sacrificing and caring for him. Now that we have become CoMamas and the years of anger and pain are over, I can truly say that my Evan is a better person for having her in his life. And just for the record, I know I am too.

Resources

Extended–Blended Family Form

The Extended-Blended Family Form is to help families develop consistent rules at both households in order to focus on putting the kids first. Start with ten simple rules you can all agree on:

1. Telephone arrangements when child is with mom and with dad
   Examples: Child calls mom at 7:00 p.m. when at dad's house on Tuesdays, Thursdays, and Saturdays. Child calls dad when at mom's house on the same days and time.
2. Holiday and special occasion schedules
3. Transportation system
4. Communication system
5. Schedule of activities for child. Who pays the expenses?
6. Educational goals and expenses
7. Medical care agreement and expenses
8. Child care arrangements and expenses
9. Emergency communications
10. Extended family visitation rules

What's Happening Form

Use this form to organize your daily and weekly schedule. Hand it directly to your stepwife or Man in the Middle, or put it in your child's backpack to take to them. Follow up by phone to make sure the plans are still on. Communicating in a timely, organized manner couldn't be easier!

WEEK OF: <u>February 17-23</u>

What's Happened?	What's Happening?	Future Dates
MONDAY		
2/17 Spelling Test B+	Soccer—bring oranges	Johnny's B-Day party 2/29
TUESDAY		
2/18 Pink Slip—didn't do math homework		Mother's day is 5/14 please call me— arrangements
WEDNESDAY		
2/19 Had a fight with friend —very upset		
THURSDAY		
2/20 The Eagles won their soccer game		
FRIDAY		
2/21 Had his physical— everything ok		
SATURDAY		
SUNDAY		

FOLLOW UP:	PHONE NUMBERS WHERE I CAN BE REACHED:

Organizations

Abuse-Excuse.com
Dean Tong
9213 Roundwood Court
Tampa, FL 33615
813-885-6173
www.abuse-excuse.com
Provides information to adults unjustly accused of child
abuse

ACFC (American Coalition for Fathers and Children)
1718 M Street, N.W., Suite 187
Washington, D.C. 20036
800-978-DADS
Nonprofit organization dedicated to keeping fathers in
their children's lives

Al Anon/Alateen Family Group Headquarters
Corporate Landing Parkway
Virginia Beach, VA 23454-5617
757-563-1600
Worldwide meeting information: 888-425-2666
www.al-anon.alateen.org
Support groups for spouses and significant adults
in an alcoholic's life and for children of
alcoholics

Alcoholics Anonymous World Services
475 Riverside Drive, 11th Floor
New York, NY 10115

212-870-3400
Provides information on alcoholism and local support
groups for the twelve-step recovery program

American Academy of Child and Adolescent Psychiatry
3615 Wisconsin Avenue, N.W.
Washington, D.C. 20016-3007
202-966-7300

American Association of Marriage and Family Therapists
1133 15th Street, N.W., Suite 300
Washington, D.C. 20005-2710
202-452-0109

American Psychological Association
750 First Street, N.E.
Washington, D.C. 20002-4242
800-324-2721

Big Brothers of America
Check local listings.

Children's Rights Council
4212 Jefferson Street
Hyattsville, MD 20781
Crcdc@erols.com
www.gocrc.com
202-547-6227
Organization dedicated to shared and equal parenting for
mothers and fathers

Dad's Divorce
11737 Administration Drive, 2nd Floor
St. Louis, MO 63146

314-993-5055
www.dadsdivorce.com
Organization dedicated to helping divorced and divorcing
fathers maximize their role in their children's lives

Kid in the Middle
121 West Monroe Avenue
St. Louis, MO 63122
314-909-9922
www.stlmo.com
Provides comprehensive affordable therapy to children and
families of divorce

Kid's Turn of San Diego
P.O. Box 868
Cardiff, CA 92007
800-878-3593
Nonprofit organization that offers workshops on child-
centered co-parenting

M.O.M.S. (Mothers on a Mission Who Are Single)
475 College Boulevard, Suite 6-176
Oceanside, CA 92075-5512
760-726-7978
www.singlemoms.org
The international nonprofit organization dedicated to
single moms and dads

National Association of Social Workers
750 First Street, N.E., Suite 700
Washington, D.C. 20002-4241
800-638-8799

National Council on Alcoholism and Drug Dependence
29 Exchange Place, Suite 2902
New York, NY 10005
national@ncadd.org, www.ncadd.org
24-hour affiliate referral: 800/NCA-CALL
Provides information and education to the public;
   advocates prevention, intervention, and treatment

National Institute of Mental Health
6001 Executive Boulevard, Room 8184, MSC 9663
Bethesda, MD 20892-9663
301-443-4513

Parents Without Partners
www.ParentsWithoutPartners.com
International nonprofit organization devoted to the
   interests of single parents and their children.

**SAA Families of the 21st Century (formerly Stepfamily
Association of America)**
650 J Street, Suite 205
Lincoln, NE 68508
800-735-0329
www.stepfam.org
A national nonprofit membership organization dedicated
   to successful stepfamily living

San Diego Family Law Council
P.O. Box 880592
San Diego, CA 92168-0592
619-234-KIDS
www.realsolutions.org/sdchildren.com

Nonprofit organization working for the success of children
living in dual-household families

Second Wives Club
4 Westwood Blvd., Unit 14, Suite 113
Upper Tantallon
Nova Scotia BZ3 1H3, Canada
www.secondwivesclub.com
Features support, resources, and advice for second wives
and stepmothers

Second Wives Crusade
22365 El Torro Road, Suite 115
Lake Forest, CA 92630
899-978-3237
www.secondwives.org
Nonprofit organization that addresses the rights of the
second wife

SMART Recovery
7537 Mentor Avenue, Suite 306
Mentor, Ohio 44060-5400
440-951-5357, fax: 440-951-5358
srmail1@aol.com, www.smartrecovery.org
Nonprofit program for alcohol abuse, drug addictions, and
substance abuse

**Substance Abuse and Mental Health Services
Administration (SAMHSA)**
5600 Fishers Lane
Rockville, MD 20857
www.info@samhsa.gov
Mental health: 301-443-0001

Substance abuse prevention: 301-443-0365
Substance abuse treatment: 301-443-5700
Provides prevention, diagnosis, and treatment services for
 substance abuse and mental illness; serves as an
 umbrella for the Center for Mental Health Services,
 Center for Substance Abuse Prevention, and Center for
 Substance Abuse Treatment

Books for Children

Two Homes, by Claire Masurel; illustrated by Kady MacDonald Denton

Dinosaurs Divorce, by Laurene Krasny Brown and Marc Brown

Changing Families: A Guide for Kids and Grown-Ups, by David Fassler, Michele Lash, and Sally Ives

The Boys and Girls Book About Divorce, by Richard A. Gardner

A Heart Full of Love, by Bette S. Margolis; illustrated by Christine L. Cline

I Love You More Than . . . , by Elizabeth Hickey and James Cohen; illustrated by Lynda Smart Brown

Daddy Day, Daughter Day, by CNN's Larry King and Chaia King; illustrated by Wendy Christensen

How to Survive Your Parents' Divorce: Kids' Advice to Kids, by Gail Kimball

I Think Divorce Stinks, by Marcia L. Lebowitz

"What Am I Doing in a Step-Family?" by Claire Berman; illustrated by Dick Wilson

It's Not Your Fault, Koko Bear: A Read-Together Book for Parents and Young Children During Divorce, by Vicki Lansky; illustrated by Jane Prince

Mom's House, Dad's House: Making Two Homes for Your Child, by Isolina Ricci, Ph.D.

Books for Children Ages 10–18

My Two Families, by Althea Braithwaite; photographs by Richard Clemence

Stepkids: A Survival Guide for Teenagers in Stepfamilies, by
Ann Getzoff and Carolyn McClenahan
Split Ends, by Ruth Webber; available from SAA Families
of the 21st Century (formerly Stepfamily Association of
America; 800-735-0329)

Notes

Chapter 8

1. Jay Folberg, "Custody Overview," in *Joint Custody and Shared Parenting,* ed. Jay Folberg (New York: Guilford Press, 1991), pp. 1-15.

2. A. M. Morrow, *Shared Custody, Financial Considerations* (Corvallis: Oregon State University, Feb. 1995), p. 3.

3. Olivia Mellan, "Men, Women, and Money," *Psychology Today* (January 1999).

4. Jessica Pearson and Nancy Thoennes, "Child Custody and Child Support After Divorce," *Joint Custody and Shared Parenting* (New York: Guilford Press, 1991), pp. 185-205.

5. "Alimony, Custody and Support," in *Divorce Law Made E-Z* (Deerfield Beach, FL: E.Z. Legal Forms, 1999), pp. 47-48.

6. Ibid., pp. 52-53.

7. Pearson and Thoennes. "Child Custody and Child Support After Divorce," p. 200

8. Laura K. Yax and Robert Berstein, "Who Receives Child Support?" Statistical Briefs. U.S. Census Bureau, Population Division. May, 1995. Sept. 13, 2000 update.

Chapter 11

1. National Institute on Alcohol Abuse and Alcoholism, *Getting the Facts About Alcohol* (1996).

2. Ibid.

3. National Institute on Alcohol Abuse and Alcoholism, *Frequently Asked Questions* (1998), p. 1; Alcoholics

Anonymous World Services, "44 Questions," Pamphlet P-2 (1952).

4. National Institute on Alcohol Abuse and Alcoholism, *The Genetics of Alcoholism* (July 1992-2000).

5. American Academy of Child and Adolescent Psychiatry, *Children of Alcoholics* No. 17, (May 1999).

6. Ibid.

7. Ibid.

8. U.S. Department of Health and Human Services, Office of Substance Abuse, "What You Can Do About Drug Use in America," DHHS Publication No. ADM 91-1572 (Rockville, MD, 1991), pp. 3-11.

9. U.S. Department of Health and Human Services. Health Resources and Services Administration. Maternal and Child Health Bureau, *Child Health USA 2000–Child Abuse and Neglect* (Washington, D.C.: U.S. Government Printing Office, 2000), p. 28.

10. American Academy of Child and Adolescent Psychiatry, *Child Sexual Abuse,* (November 1998), pp. 1-3.

11. National Institute of Mental Health, *The Numbers Count* (September 2000), pp. 1-6.

12. Ibid.

13. Judith S. Wallerstein, Julia M. Lewis, and Sandra Blakeslee, *The Unexpected Legacy of Divorce* (New York: Hyperion, 2000).

14. Symptoms summarized from the American Psychiatric Association, *Diagnostic and Statistical Manual of Mental Disorders,* 4th ed. (Washington, D.C.: American Psychiatric Association, 1994).

15. "Depression: Define It. Defeat It," available to read on the Web at www.hoptechno.com/book34.htm. Or send for "Depression: Awareness, Recognition, and Treatment,"

available from National Institute of Mental Health, Public Inquiries, Room C-05, 5600 Fishers Lane, Rockville, MD 20857.

16. National Institute of Mental Health, *The Numbers Count* (2000), p. 2.

17. Ibid.

Index

National Council on Alcoholism and
Drug Dependence, 253
National Institute of Alcohol Abuse,
225
National Institute of Mental Health,
253
negotiation skills, 137
nonverbal communication, 114-16
notes, opening communication
through, 117
nurturing, 29
of new relationships, 100
self-, 46-47, 66-67, 75, 78, 91, 105,
187, 231

obsessive-compulsive disorder, 235,
240
Old Testament, 88-89
organizations, 250-55
other woman, 82
"Over the Edge" ex-wives, 85

panic attacks, 240
paranoia, 238-39
parenting styles, 161-67
finding middle ground in, 165-67
Parents Without Partners, 109, 253
participation
in activities with children, 61
by children in caring for new
baby, 64
by stepmothers, rules about, 51
permissive parents, 164
personal history, 36-39
personality traits, 111-12
phobias, 240
phone calls, 52
by children, 160

setting limits and boundaries on,
86, 92
physical abuse, 232-33, 241
physical assaults, 86
picking up children, 160
possessions, division of, 108
posttraumatic stress disorder, 240
praise, 170
pregnancy, stepmother's, 58-59
in blended families, 63-65
PRESCRPTON, 23-48, 70, 87, 120,
125, 126, 141, 149-51, 201, 243
"Princess Bride" ex-wives, 77-79, 85
problem solving, 29, 40-42, 187
alcoholism and, 225
change and, 91
communication and, 43, 44, 111,
127
friends and, 109
by Man in the Middle, 143
styles of, 38
putting kids first, 24-26, 66, 68, 83,
89, 201, 202
in blended families, 61
communication and, 126
and Ex-Wife Envy, 104, 105
in living arrangements, 152, 159,
161
by Men in the Middle, 142
to prevent abuse, 241
in problem solving, 42
weddings and, 216

rage, *see* anger
reading aloud, 26
redefining yourself, 78
reflective listening, 43-44
remorse, divorce, 89-90